Philip F. Yuan
Lucia Phinney
Chao Yan

MATTER AGGREGATION:
A Design Studio at UVA

ORO
EDITIONS

TONGJI
UNIVERSITY
PRESS

Contents

PREFACE

INTRODUCTION

ESSAYS

PEDAGOGY

PRECEDENTIAL RESEARCH

SELECTED BUILDING PROJECTS

PREFACE

COMPUTATIONAL TECTONICS AND OTHER MATERIAL MATTERS

Ila Berman

PREFACE

Architecture is largely made up of the addition of incremental parts that aggregate into larger assemblies to such an extent that the aggregation of matter might be considered one of the most fundamental conditions of the architectural act. Whether quarried, manufactured or concocted—extracted directly from the earth or synthesized into composite substances—the cutting and molding of matter into distinctly formed discrete material elements that are then carefully conjoined and assembled is a process that hearkens back to the very origins of our discipline. Yet while the most archaic forms of building were dependent upon the simple accumulation of matter and the manner in which this matter was shaped to delimit and enclose space, the distinct ways in which material elements have been defined and the logics of their assembly have evolved in parallel with the evolution of technologies which have in turn determined the complexity of architecture's forms, substances, and modes of assemblage.

Notwithstanding the stark contrast of the digital and material realms, the immaterial ethereality of the former and perceived density of the latter, the intersection of computation, technology, and material has enabled a new trajectory to emerge within the domain of architecture—referred to by some as "digital craft"—that has continued yet complexified this longstanding history of building. In the early programmed and sequential walls of Gramazio & Kohler, for example, the introduction of robotics into the realm of architecture's standardized masonry and wood-framed wall systems—utilitarian and ideological by-products of 20th century industrialization—enabled these homogeneous assemblies of mass-produced elements to be transformed into intricate systems whose potential algorithmic variability resisted simple self-referentiality and allowed them to respond to the programmatic complexity of the environments in which they were situated. In the first two decades of the 21st century, the introduction of digital modeling, parametric design and scripting, and programmed robotic fabrication techniques, thereby allowed modern mechanistic systems, previous signifiers of the repetitive modes of industrial production, to undergo a vital morphogenesis through the absorption and material expression of local frequencies that could unfold and be smoothly distributed in relation to forces internal and external to these systems. In this process, the performative application of the ready-made—the masonry brick, concrete block or wood 2×4 for instance—became *other* to the initial trajectory of its production, transformed into a matter-vector as it was absorbed into the evolution of a larger affective whole. These modifications engendered transformations resulting in a heterogeneous system comprised of homogeneous elements, whose complexity was dependent on the variability and increased quantity of information injected into, and continuously modulated across the assemblage. Here, quality directly relied on the strategic deployment of quantity, and difference within the system was the result of changes in the mode of assembly rather than the changing form of individual elements.

MATTER AGGREGATION

As the capacities of these technologies have been amplified over the last two decades, these built assemblies have also evolved, as evidenced by the walls of *Chi She*, the Gallery of the Pond Society by Fab-Union, where robots are not simply being programmed to allow incremental variation in the wall system but are also able to be networked and imbued with sensing capacity so that they can recognize and locally respond to unanticipated feedback such as the unique characteristics of non-uniform recycled bricks.

The UVA *Matter Aggregation* studio developed by Philip F. Yuan with Lucia Phinney and Chao Yan continues this design research and its evolution by challenging students to construct larger material assemblies that expand their own design and building capacity with computational, rapid prototyping and robotic tools. Beginning with an exploration of traditional wood craftsmanship and the geometric intricacies of pre-existing joinery systems, students were encouraged to generate a customized kit of parts and language of connection between these wood elements as well as a syntax for a larger material aggregative system by determining a precise set of rules for the ways in which these basic units would be repeated, repositioned, and woven together to produce a more complex spatial assemblage. The problem that was set was not to recreate an architecture already preconceived through familiar formal and spatial typologies, but rather to create a generative machine defined through a set of procedural logics which might block in advance any possibility of predetermination. To add greater complexity to this process, students were asked to incorporate generative algorithms into their procedures that would randomly determine the sequences by which their initial joint assemblies would be conjoined and aggregated. This process generated multiple materialized hypotheses that needed to be analyzed and distilled before being structurally optimized and transformed into architectural propositions. Despite their highly tectonic origins, the first prototypes generated were thus paradoxically anti-architectural, tending to follow growth patterns that would fill rather than frame space and align more closely with natural processes of matter rather than our geometricization and instrumentalization of it. Initially scaleless and indeterminate, and procedurally generated as much by randomness as design, the material aggregates produced by this studio are thus a study in the process of formation and a way of understanding how contiguity, repetition, and spatial differentiation are fundamental to the amassing of any material architectural system.

As discussed by the authors of this project and publication, these procedures and the architectural assemblages that they might yield are also intrinsically defined by the highly complex technologies—the robots and computational algorithms—that are equally responsible for their creation, and as Philip F. Yuan has claimed, catapult us into a post-humanist world of advanced architectural exploration. As designed

8

PREFACE

machines and systems themselves, these sophisticated tools come with their own inbuilt capacities that both reflect and augment our own human sentience. In *The Body in Pain*, Elaine Scarry argues that every object "will be found to contain within its interior a material record or trace of the nature of the human life out of which it is made, and from which it in turn derives its power to act on [that life] and recreate it." That is, that we project our knowledge and capacity out into the world through and in the things that we make, and then these things—both the technologies that we use as well as the architectures that they might in turn enable us to create—have a reciprocal effect on us. These increasingly intelligent and highly communicative machines thus amplify our own performative capabilities (which we should readily embrace), not only because of the benefits of their tremendous intelligence, precision, speed, and dexterity, but also for their ability to propel us into new creative relationships with the very aggregative matters out of which architecture is made, since we make things in the world not only to remake the reality around us, but perhaps more profoundly, in order to remake ourselves.

1.   Elaine Scarry,"The Interior Structure of the
     Artifact," in *The Body in Pain* (New York:
     Oxford University Press, 1985), 280.

INTRODUCTION

MATTER AGGREGATION
A Posthumanist View on Matter and Materiality

Philip F. Yuan

INTRODUCTION

Since the end of the 20th century, two oppositional tendencies in architecture have been developing in parallel—the digital and the tectonic. While the digital tendency dissolves the ontological fundaments of the tectonic by challenging the physical nature of architectural space, the latter was against the pure interest in plasticity and, particularly, the inconsistency between form and structure in the early experiments of the digital in architecture.

Emerged from the efforts to fill the gap between the digital and the tectonic, the term "digital tectonics" was adopted by many scholars and architects to address the capabilities of then newly evolved digital tools to model the material properties of architectural components[1]. However, as many criticisms pointed out, the early efforts only celebrated a new paradigm of design thinking which referred to the computational structural performance, but failed to explicit the expressive nature of the digitally created tectonics in correlation with human experience[2].

Within these contexts, this studio seeks new materiality for the contemporary digital design and fabrication of architecture. Following the contemporary revived tectonic culture in the age of architectural robotics, digital crafts are playing an increasingly important role in forming various ways of matter aggregation for architecture. Meanwhile, as the traditional media of correlating tectonics, structure and construction, crafts are also essential to the formation of architectural meaning and the expression of architectural spatiality.

In the scenario of the automated production of architectural robotics, crafts themselves have also undergone a cognitive shift. Instead of merely mediating human and material, crafts in the age of automation also cultivates a dialog among matters without the intervention of human beings. By readdressing matter aggregation in association with the notion of automation, the dialog between emerging digital technologies, material culture and crafts could open the possibilities for forming new materiality and unprecedented spatial affects. In this way, matter aggregation is not only a new methodological approach to pursue architectural materiality in the age of the digital, but also an epistemological paradigm towards the posthumanist future in architectural design and production. This essay will mainly focus on elaborating some of key notions of this posthumanist view of matter aggregation.

In ancient China, the interrelationship between human and surrounding world has been implicated in Taoist philosophy. As one of its profounding reflection in architecture, traditional Chinese Garden is not only a physical space for recreative activities, but also an ideal space that reflects a harmonic relationship between human body and nature. *Yuan Ye*, China's first garden art theory monograph, introduced the idea of borrowing scenery and blending into surrounding environment, which emphasized the connection between human beings and nature. Garden is not isolated from human inhabitant, but is regarded as an extension of the limited human space, forming continued connections between human and the dwelling world. The notion of the borrowing scenery has already revealed a posthumanist version of inhabitation.

In contemporary, there is also a kind of the posthumanist tendency in the Western philosophy as well. The works by contemporary philosophers like Bernard Stiegler, Benjamin Bratton, et al., have potentially formed a more holistic view toward the world, which gives us an general perspective to posit ourselves into the world and to understand our relationship to it with a more modest attitude.

In this context, a new design paradigm shall be discussed, which states the end of anthropocentric era and the beginning of post humanism in architecture. Certainly, human would continue to play an important role in the design and construction of architecture, and be responsible for genuinely creative activities. But is this state sustainable? There is no indication that the creativity of nature or machines will approach a limit, neither the other hyperobjects will approach one. Also, it is noticeable that human may not be the only dominant group regarding to the inhabitation in the built environment. There are buildings not designed for humans, but for other entities much bigger than us, a hyperobject, in Timothy Morton's term.

Hyperobjects is the concept firstly introduced by Timothy Morton in *The Ecological Thought*, and later elaborated in *Hyperobjects: Philosophy and Ecology after the End of the World*. According to him, hyperobjects refer to the things that are so massively distributed in time and space that its existence beyond human cognition[3], such as the biosphere, solar system, nuclear waste, global warming, capitalism, and real estate investments, etc. In his book, the term refers to an alternative thinking paradigm and methodology, towards the issues and crises in the Anthropocene. For example, in the ecological system, the reality of a hyperobject is withdrawn and independent from our imagination, but its existence has tremendous impacts. Therefore, for example, we need to place ourselves in a humbler position in dealing with ecological issues, to take a posthumanist attitude in rethinking our relationship with the world.

When applying the concept into architecture, there is a question raised by Peter Trummer: is architecture necessarily designed for human and by human? In the context of hyperobjects, the answer is obviously no. As Peter Trummer has articulated, the architecture in the age of hyperobjects could be designed for something bigger than human self, such as

INTRODUCTION

some of the "green building" are not actually built for human, but for the whole eco-system[4]. Also, the architectural hyperobjects could also have their own autonomy in terms of creation. Design doesn't have to begin with abstractions in human mind in order to produce real things, but instead directly merges real objects to generate new entities. In that case, architectures are designed with either object-and-object or object-and-machine.

The thesis of the hyperobject allow us to see beyond the human-centered built environment for the first time. What happens if we think of the architectures first from the perspective of a nonhuman subject? What can we learn from the architecture aggregated as a hyperobject?

To better explain the idea of hyperobject in association with architectural matter and materiality, we need to revisit its core concepts in the original construction. According to Timothy Morton, hyperobjects have three properties in common—nonlocal, viscous and interobjectivity. Nonlocal means that hyperobjects have a high-dimensional space with invisible qualities. Any "local manifestation" of a hyperobject is not directly the hyperobject. Viscous refers to "sticking" to beings that are involved with them. Interobjectivity means hyperobjects can be detected in a space that consists of interrelationships between aesthetic properties of objects[5].

In architecture, nonlocal lies in the emphasis on form-finding over form-making, on bottom-up over top-down processes, and formation rather than form. Indeed, the term "form" itself should be relegated to a sub-position to the term "formation". Meanwhile, "formation" must be recognized as being linked to the qualities related to information and performance in a higher dimensional space. When architecture is "informed" by performative considerations it becomes less a consideration of formal appearance in and of itself, and more a latent process of material formations. In short, nonlocality refers to the invisible qualities of hyperobjects in the high-dimensional levels. So, we need to understand architectural hyperobjects not only in their extrinsic geometry, but also their intrinsic quality–material performance.

In terms of nonlocality, designing an architectural hyperobject is also to conceive architecture as an aggregated material system in responding to other systems, such as social, cultural, and environmental systems. Those systems are so massively distributed that are beyond human cognition. Thus, we use computers to simulate, visualize the internal mechanism of each system in order to generate architectural form accordingly with its performance in each system. By that, architectural design would become a performance-based generative process, which consists of simulation, visualization, generation, iteration, optimization and fabrication.

MATTER AGGREGATION

With this integrated production process, we have been exploring and re-understanding materiality from the perspective of human-machine collaboration in recent years. In the past three years, we have built a series of bridges to experiment on the process.

The form of each bridge is generated based on its structural performance. Firstly, by setting the start and end points, and the value of applied loads, structural simulation software, like Kangaroo, could help the architect to find the basic geometry of the bridges. Then, another set of digital tools, like Millipede and Ameba, could be introduced to optimize the structure by removing the useless material in the bridge. From form-finding to form optimization, an iterative feedback loop of design could be established to approach the best way of aggregating material together.

Particularly regarding to the bridge constructed during the DigitalFUTURES 2019 workshop, Tongji University collaborated with Fab-Union, combining two robotic fabrication techniques—filament winding and large-scale 3D metal printing—with structural optimization tools. This bridge spans 11.4 meters, rises 3.9 meters, connecting the ground floor and the basement. With millimeter construction precision, the main structure thickness tapers from only 20 centimeters. Through the collaboration with XIE Technologies, typology optimization software based on BESO (Bi-Directional Evolutionary Structural Optimization) was used to optimize the structure performance. As a result, the main structure is weight only around 450 kilograms, and capable of holding up more than 20 people.

Back to the second property, viscous refers to the merging relationship between hyperobjects, which suggests that architectural hyperobjects would also have the continuity in their interrelationships. The process of performance-based design is framed in a viscous environment, in which every hyperobject is dynamically connected with others. And as each architectural hyperobject is an intrinsic system, their viscous relationship would cause the continuous transition between each system, forming multiplicity, dynamicity and uncertainty of the environment. Eventually, architecture becomes an immersive environment that cultivates ambiguous and affective dialogs with its inhabitants.

Meanwhile, from the perspective of the notion of viscous, technology is not in conflict with culture, but merged with each other continuously. Digital fabrication should not only be interpreted as a building technology, but also as an inherent measure in cultural aspects like building materials, crafts and architectural industry. The discourse in the digital age has cultivated new social and ethical significance. In the past few years, we've been trying to implement the fabrication technology into this new social and cultural scenario. The Chi She project, also known as the gallery of the Pond Society, shows that digital technology, history and culture can

Figure 1

Fab-Union and the DDRC of Tongji University, Robotic Plastic Printing Bridge, Shanghai, 2017; Fab-Union and the DDRC of Tongji University, Robotic Metal Printing Bridge, Shanghai, 2018; Fab-Union and the DDRC of Tongji University, Robotic Fiber Winding Bridge, Shanghai, 2019

Figure 2

Hybrid Structure of the Robotic Fiber Winding Bridge

MATTER AGGREGATION

Figure 3

Fab-Union,
Chi She (Pond
Society),
Shanghai, 2016

Figure 4

Fab-Union,
Robotic Factory,
Shanghai, 2015

INTRODUCTION

be compatible. It is a story of harmoniously combining advanced robotic brick masonry and historic traces. In this project, Form is not just the "looking", but also implicating invocations of traditions and nostalgia. This project used in-situ robots to fabricate. The sensors on the robots are able to scan, recognize and provide real-time feedback from the unique characteristic of each non-standard recycle brick, which helps to precisely place each brick to achieve the global geometric form.

The automatic construction technology in Chi She project brings us to the last notion of hyperobject—interobjectivity, meaning that the interrelationships between hyperobjects could be independent from human beings. Therefore, the production process of an architectural hyperobjects could also build upon a hybrid authorship[6]. The interobjectivity of hyperobjects could form a view of architectural production based on automation and machine intelligence. The architectural hyperobject is not only conceived, iterated, and fabricated by human beings, but could also by other hyperobjects—the computer and the robots. We need interpret tools and crafts as containing their own agency. Their direct dialog with materials could generate new entities of architectural hyperobjects. In this way, the changing authorship of architectural production cultivates a posthumanist paradigm of architectural design and fabrication towards human-machines collaborations.

With industrial robots as the revolutionary construction platform in the digital era, the architectural profession is experiencing a great paradigm shift from traditional crafts and industrial reproduction to cyborg craftsmanship techniques. Following the hardware development and processing techniques, we developed FUROBOT software to integrate the flow of architectural geometry design, performance-based simulation, and parametric fabrication. It can connect the design and fabrication process on the platform of KUKA, ABB and UR robots, which has been extremely useful in various scenarios such as robotic timber fabrication, 3D printing and brick-laying craftsmanship. As a robot programming platform for architectural construction industry, FUROBOT aims to connect the design process with the fabrication process seamlessly, so that designers and fabricators could more simply engage into the robot fabrication. The robotic simulation and programming module are developed in C#, which could be easily connecting to any parametric design platform. Furthermore, FUROBOT has inherited all the process accumulations from the experience of Archi-Union and Fab-Union in the last ten years, which can help users to realize the rapid development of different fabrication scenarios.

As a representative outcome of FUROBOT-involved robotic fabrication, the Red Pavilion starts from the traditional form-finding of brick structure, and is further optimized through advanced digital algorithm design to generate an ultra-thin structure under pure compression. It is a large-scale brick shell with complicated geometry generated by the 3D equilibrium of compressive structural action, with a built-in 3D printed formwork system. The design of the geometry applied the Thrust Network Analysis method and the tool RhinoVAULT to generate the compression-only thrust lines. To avoid a great waste of formwork system, a reciprocal formwork system with 1,500 3D-printed blocks was designed for the construction of the shell. Together with a polyurethane insulation layer which is milled with the robotic arms, the formwork system works permanently as part of the architecture. The prefabrication of all the blocks was finished in-house with 7 robotic arms and post-processed with the following sequences including the installation of the isolating layer with glass-fiber fabric and the casting and milling of the PU insulation layer.

Within the continuous design-to-construction process of the bridge, we realized that contemporary architects are inseparable from machines, both virtual and actual. From structural optimization tool to automatic construction tool, machines are kind of hyperobjects, whose operation and collaboration are running parallel with human subject. So, we must not only think about the relationship between humans and machines, but also things and things, which is briefly explained as performance-based design here.

In a posthumanist production mode, digital design and construction has been developed to acquire a new understanding of the matter and materiality in architecture[7]. The subject of matter aggregation is extended beyond a materialization process to an indication of the automated generation process from design to construction, as well as the dynamic relationship between human and nonhuman agencies involved in the whole production system. The new way of design-to-construction indicated by matter aggregation should not only be interpreted in association with finding new forms, but also as an approach to bring other systems (cultural, social, economic, etc.) into architecture from a posthuman perspective. In that sense, fabricating an architecture object becomes to fabricate a hyperobject, an object, according to Timothy Morton, that is massively distributed in time and space relative to humans. Fabrication as well as architecture would become an entity moving beyond individual physical object, beyond individual human cognition, eventually, to be immersive with our social networks, our cultural context, and our natural environment.

Figure 5
(right page)
Fab-Union, the Red Pavilion of Wuzhen Internet Conference, Wuzhen, Zhejiang, 2019

MATTER AGGREGATION

1. Neil Leach, David Turnbull, and Chris Williams, eds., *Digital Tectonics* (London: Wiley-Academy, 2004), 4-13.

2. Jean Pierre Chupin, "The 'Tectonic Bug' (The Fall of the Body in Cyberspace) —Current and Recurrent Tensions between the Virtual and the Tectonic," *The Proceedings of SIGradi 2004* (São Leopoldo: Universidade do Vale do Rio dos Sinos, 2004), 493-500.

3. Timothy Morton, *The Ecological Thought* (Cambridge: Harvard University Press, 2010).

4. Peter Trummer, "Architecture in the Age of Hyperobjects," *Log* (Winter/Spring 2019): 35-42.

5. Timothy Morton, *Hyperobjects: Philosophy and Ecology after the End of the World* (Minneapolis, MN: University of Minnesota Press, 2013).

6. Mario Carpo, *The Alphabet and the Algorithm* (Cambridge: The MIT Press, 2001).; Wendy W. Fok and Antoine Picon, eds., "Digital Property: Open-source Architecture (Special Issue)." *Architectural Design* 86 (September/October 2016).

7. Antoine Picon, "Architecture and the Virtual: Towards a New Materiality," *Praxis* no.6 (2004): 114-121.

ESSAYS

MATTER AGGREGATION AS GROWTH

Lucia Phinney

ESSAYS

The work of the *Matter Aggregation* Studio is situated within a history of thought and experimentation across a wide historical and intellectual territory. These notes about the nature and intentions embedded in this territory can help to describe the meaning of this work and suggest some potential outcomes of further explorations.

D'Arcy Thompson, Noam Chomsky, Aristid Lindenmayer, George Stiny, and James Gips

The potential to design in the mode of nature has been a continuing thread in the history of architecture. This interest has been present since the first treatise on architecture by Vitruvius, and has continued with such divergent approaches as *An Essay on Architecture* by Marc-Antoine Laugier (1753) with its powerful illustration of the primitive hut and the *Vers Une Architecture of Le Corbusier* (1923). However, it was D'Arcy Thompson's *On Growth and Form*, published in 1917 with its vastly expanded edition of 1942 that was the first approach to value the most crucial characteristics of nature, its capacity for self-generating growth and change. Thompson's inventive transformational diagrams and the accompanying mathematical descriptions have been and continue to be a provocation especially in the realm of sophisticated computational architecture. The title is notable: linking form—the architectural domain, with growth—the domain of nature. From Thompson's mathematical illustrations of cell-packing; to the mathematics of radiolaria configurations; to the branching cell structures of plants; and to the relationships revealed by the scaling, extending, compressing, and shearing of animal structures through which the differences in the forms of related animals could be described by mathematical transformations, D'Arcy Thompson's work continues to inspire architects.

In this context, a further elucidation of Thompson's studies of plant cell growth patterns was introduced by the Hungarian theoretical biologist Aristid Lindenmayer as L-Systems in 1968. Lindenmayer's formal grammar consists of "an alphabet of *symbols* that can be used to make strings, a collection of production rules that expand each symbol into some larger string of symbols, an initial *axiom* string from which to begin construction, and a mechanism for translating the generated strings into geometric structures"[1]. The L-System uses the concept of *rewriting*, a technique in which one starts with a simple object and uses a system of rudimentary rules to define successive additions of this object, ultimately creating a surprisingly complex form from such simple beginnings. Lindenmayer's work, though within the field of botany, was initiated in the larger context of a wide resurgence of interest in string rewriting. This new interest had been catalyzed with the publication of *Syntactic Structures* (1957), linguist Noam Chomsky's work on formal transformational grammar[2]. Chomsky had applied the concept of rewriting to describe the syntactic features of natural languages. His transformational grammar was an analytic tool for understanding languages, yet Chomsky went further to see it as a generative element in language. If language is shaped by a set of basic principles that underlie the human ability to speak and understand, then generative grammar implies a creative process with two goals: that the grammar could be learned, and that it could evolve. Again, it is notable that simple rules and transformational operations were shown to be behind the most complex and sophisticated system of communication: human speech.

While Lindenmayer was working computationally with L-Systems to produce the work that grew into *The Algorithmic Beauty of Plants*[3], George Stiny and James Gips were similarly inspired by Chomsky's work in linguistics. In their 1971 presentation to the International Federation of Information Processing Societies in Ljubljana, Slovenia[4], they proposed the idea of shape grammar, as a graphic counterpart to Chomsky's transformational grammar. In their presentation they state that "where phrase structure grammars are defined over an alphabet of symbols and generate one-dimensional strings of symbols, shape grammars are defined over an alphabet of shapes and generate multi-dimensional shapes."[5] Their shape grammar includes: 1) shape rules that specify how a shape may be transformed, 2) a generation engine that iteratively selects and applies transformations, and 3) a termination rule to end the generation process. Stiny and Gips conceived of shape grammars "as a formal, generative technique to produce good art objects and to develop understanding of what makes good art objects."[6] Therefore, following Chomsky, they understood shape grammar to be both analytic and creative.

This cutting-edge work in linguistics, botany, art from fifty years ago holds great potential for architecture. Shape grammar has produced notable results when used to study such diverse architectural topics as Palladian grammar, Mughal gardens, ancient Chinese buildings, Frank Lloyd Wright's Prairie Houses, and the work of Glenn Murcutt. Yet, until very recently, most of the architectural attention to this arena has been directed more toward the analytic project than the generative one. Peter Eisenman, starting with his earliest houses, stands out as an exception to this tendency. His work has great historical import, and also holds intriguing clues for the generative project.

Peter Eisenman and Chris Yessios

While the development of computers and computer languages provided a foundation for Chomsky, Lindenmayer, Stiny, and Gips, one might claim that the non-computational work of Peter Eisenman was just as important. In the 1960s, Peter Eisenman pursued architectural experiments that were distinct from other architects practicing at the time. Although he had a wide circle of friends and collaborators, Eisenman was the only architect who developed his spatial ideas through sequential generative diagrams. As with Lindenmayer, Stiny, and Gips, the logic behind these diagrams was inspired by the contemporaneous work of Noam Chomsky. Already, in the early 1960s, Eisenman was known for his emphasis on syntax. In his 1963 essay "Towards an Understanding of Form in Architecture", he reasoned that "architecture is in essence the giving of form."[7] He raised form to a position of primacy among essential architectural elements: intent (or concept), function, structure, and technics. With the idea that only form is able to order the total environment of architecture, he developed a language of form—independent of outside meaning—to ensure that his work was grounded in logic. This was a system of formal procedures and transformational rules, similar to Chomsky's linguistic syntax.

To create a spatial syntax, Eisenman could apply ideas from the artist Sol LeWitt, who in turn, had (famously)[8] been inspired by the early 19th century photographer and pioneering kinesiologist Eadweard Muybridge. Muybridge had studied human and animal movement through serial photography. LeWitt viewed this serialization as a way to explore the structural principles of a grid, finding "extraordinary richness in systematic formal logic, developing complex structures out of the simplest elements such as a two-by-two grid with lines in four directions."[10] One can immediately intuit the specific connection to Eisenman's diagrammatic process in LeWitt's Serial Project, I (ABCD) from 1966.[9] Eisenman's earliest work was published in *Five Architects: Eisenman, Graves, Gwathmey, Hejduk, Meier*[10]. From his diagrams in this publication, one can infer that his architectural grammar was initiated from a series of horizontal and vertical planar transformations, which, through extrusion and volumetric subtraction, created spatial patterns. These might resemble columns, beams, walls, floors, and ceilings, yet primarily would be understood as form rather than structure. According to Eisenman, form should be seen as the primary outcome with function and structure as a secondary consequence of planar operations, as if it were a coincidence that some spaces could be used as passages or storage spaces, and that some of the columns might be structurally significant. As with Chomsky, he conceived of this serial process as a generative and open-ended syntax. Eisenman produced his diagrams with precision in terms of the exact sequence and the legibility of details. The diagrams, as linguistic generators were as important as the built outcome. The houses were to be valued as constructed examples of a set of possibilities that might arise from this architectural language. Regarding House II, Eisenman notes: These diagrams describe the development of a set of abstract formal propositions as a possible condition of an underlying structure and their initial transformation into a specific environment.[11]

As we have seen, the idea of starting with one or two simple objects and then sequentially following a simple set of transformational rules to generate complexity was used by Chomsky in linguistics, Lindenmayer in botany, and in graphic art by Stiny and Gips. This idea has been applied with great and wide-ranging success by Stephen Wolfram, who discovered a series of fundamental connections between computation and nature quite early in his multi-faceted career in mathematics and science. One of his key insights was that simple programs may not do simple things [that is, they may do complex things]. He notes: "Even from very simple programs, behavior of great complexity could emerge."[12] When Wolfram's ideas are directed to the extreme complexity of the rapidly urbanizing informal settlements of the world, this complexity can now be taken to mean that a small number of implicit rules, when followed, may be sufficiently powerful to create the conditions for sustainable growth.

In 1987, Peter Eisenman had an opportunity to collaborate with Chris Yessios, a computer scientist at Ohio State University, to test Wolfram's idea regarding simple rules. With Eisenman's suggested software amplifications, they employed a precursor of the Yessios computer graphic program Form Z[13] for the Biozentrum Competition, an addition to Goethe University in Frankfurt am Main. This elegant project specified four different elements, each of which—in a sequence of operations—could be scaled and attached to each other at a location specified by a point and an angle of incidence. Eisenman explains: "The shapes of the inner faces of these figures [proteins] are capable of locking together in pairs… The project articulates the three most basic processes by which DNA produces proteins: replication, transcription, and translation." Yessios stated that, contrary to the standard architectural practice at the time, the design team "quickly agreed (or was persuaded by Eisenman) that the problem was not one of arranging spaces and securing appropriate and sufficient linkages. It was rather a problem of designing the generative process."[14] The sequence of operations, selected by a type of generation engine, was arbitrary, but the rules governing the connections were defined. The random aspect, introduced through the arbitrary sequence, was a key aspect of the project. As described in Greg Lynn's interview with Eisenman in 2013, in viewing many iterations, Eisenman was able to choose the one with the optimum spatial outcome. Further, the ability to view many iterations prompted Eisenman to request even more iterations in hopes of finding an improved outcome. In particular, he was looking for a volumetric, or figure/figure spatial reading.[15]

The Matter Aggregation Studio

The foundational work outlined above provided grounding for the 2019 Matter Aggregation Studio at the University of Virginia. With a studio brief and leadership by Philip F. Yuan of Tongji University, co-teaching with Lucia Phinney from the University of Virginia, the students were given the challenge to design an art gallery for the Westbund Arts District of Shanghai. They were instructed to define this structure through inventive use of a simple kit of elements connected by joints derived from traditional Chinese or Japanese architecture. The studio work proceeded in a sequence of stages. As in the concept of rewriting, common to Chomsky's transformational grammar, L-Systems, and shape grammar, the students started with one or two objects and used a system of rules to define successive additions to each object. They chose wood shapes as their elements, then carefully researched a selection of traditional joints to be cut from the elements. They applied rules that specified a point/ vector combination, defining how each element could be connected. Then, having displayed their understanding of the basic shape grammar through detailed drawings of an initial sequence of a few iterations, the students were encouraged to move ahead with a new software package, the Wasp plugin[16] for the popular visual scripting language, Grasshopper. Wasp became the "generation engine that iteratively selected and applied transformations". In this case, massive, dense aggregations were iterated, sufficient for defining an entire building.

It is notable that while rules prescribed how the elements were connected by joints, the exact order in which this was done was randomly chosen by the Wasp software. This meant that each iteration had the potential to produce a unique outcome, distinct from other iterations. In other words, a random element was embedded in the process, so that the result was stochastic rather than deterministic. The students could run through hundreds of iterations and then make a choice. To make this choice, the students were looking for a volumetric, or figure/figure spatial reading. There was the potential that they could discover this quality among the iterations. For example, they might find a random solution that happened to suggest volumes for necessary entries, pathways, service elements, galleries, etc. Alternatively, the students could define secondary rules to push the process toward a preferred result. This was easily possible through accessory scripts in the Wasp software that, for instance, keep elements from populating areas within defined boundaries. Finally, the students could decide to introduce deterministic Grasshopper scripts to create aggregations for highly specific functions such as stairs and furniture. At the end of this process of iteration, selection, testing of secondary rules, and additional deterministic scripting, the outcome of the project could be a remarkably consistent work of architecture, designed and constructed within a single shape grammar.[17]

It is important to note the significance of the stochastic, or random element. This is a significant challenge to the longstanding, but often implicit understanding of coherency and completion in architecture that has been based on Leon Battista Alberti's 15th Century definition of beauty in art, specifying that "Beauty is that reasoned harmony of all the parts within a body, so that nothing may be added, taken away, or altered, but for the worse."[18] Here, Alberti is arguing for completion and finality. This idea of completion is possible through a deterministic solution, a process that leads to a single outcome, whereas a stochastic process is open and therefore yields "a pattern that may be analyzed statistically but may not be predicted precisely".[19] It is this open and generative process that counterintuitively is better able to accommodate the natural forces and flows of an ecological, social, cultural and political context.

An Open Process

This studio became a critique of the normative design process, which typically looks to a set of prescriptive guides that value the completed artifact and not the process, leading to a static formal outcome for a building, in spite of finding itself in the midst of an active site with a dynamic of physical, social, and environmental forces. By contrast, this studio starts with a joint. Conceptually this joint is an immaterial description of potential connection that bring together the disparate pieces that will eventually constitute an active, animated structure that is part of a living and evolving context. It obviously must be added to, taken away from and altered, all for the better. As applied at all scales of design it is integral to a living building process, continually capable of being re-imagined as new conditions and new generations present themselves.

ESSAYS

1. https://en.wikipedia.org/wiki/L-system.

2. Przemyslaw Prusinkiewicz, Aristid Lindenmayer The Algorithmic Beauty of Plants http://algorithmicbotany.org/papers/abop/ abop.pdf p.2.

3. Note that the key people in this essay- Aristid Lindenmayer, George Stiny and James Gips, Peter Eisenman, Sol LeWitt, and Chris Yessios- all list Noam Chomsky as a major influence for their work.

4. http://algorithmicbotany.org/papers/abop/ abop.pdf.

5. http://www.cs.bc.edu/~gips/ ShapeGrammarsIFIPS71.pdf.

6. http://www.cs.bc.edu/~gips/ ShapeGrammarsIFIPS71.pdf pp 4-5.

7. Peter Eisenman, *Eisenman Inside Out: Selected Writing 1963-1988* (New Haven: Yale University Press, 2004),5.

8. https://www.nytimes.com/1991/07/21/arts/ art-view-peering-into-peepholes-and-finding-politics.html.

9. https://artmuseum.williams.edu/ sol-lewitt-the-well-tempered-grid/.

10. Collection of the Museum of Modern Art, New York City https://www.moma.org/collection/ works/81533.

11. Peter Eisenman et al., *Five Architects: Eisenman, Graves, Gwathmey, Hejduk, Meier* (Oxford: Oxford University Press, 1975).

12. Stephen Wolfram, *A New Kind of Science* (Champaign: Wolfram Media, 2002), 19.

13. "The roots of Form Z go back to Yessios' doctoral thesis of 1973, entitled: "Syntactic Structures and Procedures for Computable Site Planning", for which he developed a language that automated space planning, based on the use of shape grammars. The generation of form through pre-given shapes capitalized on Noam Chomsky's generative grammars."

14. Ingeborg Rocker, "Architectures of the Digital Realm: Experimentations by Peter Eisenman | Frank Gehry," *Die Realit{ä}t Des Imagin{ä}ren 120* (2008): 249–62. https://e-pub.uni-weimar.de/opus4/frontdoor/deliver/ index/docId/1332/file/rocker_pdfa.pdf.

15. "The Foundations of Digital Architecture: Peter Eisenman" interview by Greg Lynn May 21, 2013 https://www.youtube.com/ watch?v=hKCrepgOix4.

16. The developer of Wasp is Andrea Rossi, an architectural researcher and computational designer. He is currently a Research Associate at EDEK, University of Kassel. https://ddu-research.com/wasp-plugin-for-grasshopper/#:~:text=Wasp%20is%20a%20set%20 of,and%20discrete%20design%20at%20DDU.

17. An account of this studio cannot be complete without offering a note of thanks to Kengo Kuma and Gilles Retsin for their adventurous work with aggregations, and to Andrea Rossi for developing the Wasp plugin.

18. Leon Battista Alberti, *On the Art of Building in Ten Books (Book 6)*. trans. Joseph Rykwert, Neil Leach, and Robert Tavernor (Cambridge: The MIT Press, 1988), 156.

19. *Oxford English Dictionary*, Second Edition, Volume XVI (Oxford: Clarendon Press, 1989), 730.

DIGITAL CRAFTS
Rethinking Tools in Digital Design and Pedagogy

Chao Yan

ESSAYS

If technology is recognized as one of the main factors driving the transformation of architecture, it would be even more true in the contemporary context with the rapid development of digital technology. The past 30 years has witnessed the myriad ways in which digital technology has cultivated significant paradigm shifts in architectural research, pedagogy and practice. The constant iteration of digital tools has continuously changed the way architects work. On the one hand, through the seamless transfer of geometric information between digital tools, architectural design and construction are reintegrated into reciprocal work flow, which not only breaks the boundaries between virtual and material, but also reconstructs the order from design to construction. With the help of information modeling tools and rapid prototyping tools, architects can constantly switch between virtual design and material construction. On the other hand, as automation technology matures, architectural design and construction tools begin to challenge the traditional definition of architects as the only creative subject. The generative design software and CNC machines have become the extension of the architect's brain and body, forming a working mode of human-machine symbiosis. In this context, the notion of digital crafts for the integration of human and tools has gradually emerged in the digital age.

Digital Technology as an Extension of Human Creativity

With industrial robots and digital software as its revolutionary platforms, we can see a clear transformation of the production process of architecture away from traditional crafts and industrial reproduction to a new production mode within our emerging digital age. From ancient times to the Middle Ages, buildings were constructed by artisans and master builders working on the actual construction site. Since the Renaissance, drawing as the notational tool has divorced the architect from the physical process of construction[1]. Later, through divisions of labor in the modern era, on-site building construction was replaced by industrial prefabrication and assembly lines. This evolution has resulted in an industrial deskilling whereby architects have gradually lost the knowledge and skills associated with direct building construction. In the digital age, the development of digital tools cultivated a new mode of production being fundamentally different from the discrete process of design—draw—build, this new mode of production has sought to reconnect architects and construction, reinstating architects as the master-builder in the digital age.

In this new mode of production, the digital tools are not only tools of making, but also tools of thinking. According to the philosopher Andy Clark, as human beings we are ourselves natural-born cyborgs. It is precisely our capacity to adapt to new tools that they become absorbed within our body schemas[2]. And as Katherine Hayles articulates, if the mutual intervention between human and tool in the 19th and early 20th century

33

was still mechanical rather than informational, it would be only through the 1960s, when the media of the informational exchange was increased, that tool began to be recognized as the prostheses connecting and fabricating the body virtually[3]. In that sense, the incessant development of increasingly sophisticated digital tools—from robotic platforms to artificial intelligence— have been making us ever more cyborg-like. As the user, we will gradually change our design thinking in the process of adapting to the character and prerogatives of digital technology.

In this way, digital technology not only improves the dynamicity of communication between design and construction, it also provides entirely new perspective to understand innovation and creation. Through the process of making—the intuitive dialog between human and material, the creativity within the medieval crafts once again becomes the central topic in understanding architectural design. However, in this digitally structured process of making, the essence of creativity is no longer limited to the mere energy and contours of the human hand. It now includes an array of intelligent machines capable of extending human intentions outward, away from the body. In this human–machine collaboration, applications of digital tools and robotics are not limited to visualizations and realizations of the conceived form by human subjects, but can be involved directly in the creation process and become a source of creativity in itself. No longer is the human the only author of an architectural project. Machines are also part of the design subject, forming a new mixed subjective in the creation process. In this way, new possibilities for collaboration between human and machine question traditional design authorship and challenge the traditional concept of the creative genius[4].

Reinventing Tools in Design Process

In a contemporary practice built upon human–machine collaboration, the object-centered production mode also undergoes a significant transformation. Because technology always contains a certain functional affordance to enframe, in Heidegger's word, a particular way of using[5], new tools for architectural design and construction should be constantly invented and reinvented in order to seek new ways of conceptualizing and realizing complex forms. Shifting this focus has resulted in radically new scenarios of architectural authorship and ownership. Architects are not only credited for offering building designs, but also the tools producing them[6].

In the architectural design process in association with this new scenario, the focuses could include inventing new tools and procedures in parallel with exploring formal languages and styles. The processes, interfaces and systems of design-to-construction technologies could be customized or modified according to the intention of design. Tools could become active to drive the creation process rather than being merely a passive precondition of the design. Tools could be invented, inventively used or even misused in order to stimulate new creativity. The collaboration between architects and tools will become highly differentiated and could cultivate diversified design results.

Meanwhile, as elaborated in the last section, inventing new tools is not only about expanding methods of generating and fabricating architectural objects, but also concerned with cultivating a new context of understanding the central nature of design, creativity and even architecture itself. As the human-machine collaboration has been increasingly challenging the definition of creativity, architectural design could be rethought in a totally different way in its association with those new tools. Fundamental to this process will be the mutual influential relationship between design thinking and design tools. The key question will point at how they would determine each other in this increasingly intricate human-machine collaboration.

To rethink design tools in an active sense of forming design thinking, the philosophy of technology also play essential roles in architectural design. If general architectural history and theory help us to reconstruct the creative process of the existing building so as to conceive and criticize a new one, then, the philosophy of technology should help us to unfold the existing relationship between human and technical tools in order to form new perspectives. Technology would no longer be taken for granted, but would be re-conceptualized as something to be constantly criticized and reimagined in association with the iteration of design thinking.

Design Pedagogy in the Age of Digital Crafts

With the new tool thinking in the age of digital crafts, architectural design pedagogy is also undergoing essential changes. Tools for generative design and experimental digital fabrication have gradually become an important part of design studio, and a large number of experimental installations have emerged in recent years. This new learning mode not only re-emphasizes the importance of materiality in architectural design, but also enables students to get rid of the limitations of past design techniques through the collaboration between humans and machines, inspiring a new way of conceiving space in the context of digitalization. In a design pedagogy within the context of digital crafts, the key is not only to associate various digital tools with design process, but also to explore how to use those tools as the driving factors to stimulate students' creativity in conceiving architectural space.

In the integrated design and construction mode under human-machine collaboration, digital tools have formed a new mutual determination relationship between body, craft and tool in the process of dealing with material. And it has gradually eliminated the gap between digitally produced form and human sensibility in the earlier stage of digital design exploration. Now, tectonics, structure, and construction are becoming the primary subjects in association with digital tools. If we interpret architecture as an assembly of material elements that have made of sub-assemblies of material elements, then the aim of digital design and construction will become to conceive a particular way of assembling those material elements together.

As the embodiment of the construction process, tectonics can be understood as the most basic unit of architectural assembly. In architecture, tectonics represent the joint method of two or more basic building components. By aggregating the joint through hierarchical or flat iterations, it eventually constitutes the whole building system. Based on this interpretation, collaborating with automated design tools could get rid of the traditional top-down design conception, and turn into a bottom-up form-finding method through the iterations of the assemblies of architectural elements, forming a hybrid creativity between students and design tools. Meanwhile, unlike the traditional generative design that usually begins with abstract form, the design method of digital craft method introduces material properties and physical limitations of the assembly process, so that the generated architectural prototype is not only formal but also structural. Students no longer operate on abstract forms, but always embody the perception of material in the process of conceiving architectural space.

In understanding architectural materiality, tectonics have been always addressed in correspondence with both construction and structure. According to Eduard F. Sekler, their relationship could be explained as such: structure, the intangible concept, is realized through construction and given visual expression through tectonics[7]. In that sense, tectonics— the joints of the basic elements—are directly corresponded to the flow of the force in the overall form of architectural assembly. Then, due to the randomness of the bottom-up assembly process, the generated architectural assembly will usually show the redundancy of components. Therefore, during the design process in respecting to the specific context, students usually need to optimize the overall form to fulfill the internal and external demands of the project. This optimization process may not only aim at the efficiency and rationality of the structure, but also construct the adaptability of the space to other aspects such as social, cultural, economic, etc. However, in the optimization process, the essential criteria are still relying on the understanding of the materiality of the assembly in respect to its structural capability. Only by retaining the load-bearing elements to fulfill the basic structural requirement, the optimization operations could achieve certain flexibility in correlation to the dynamic equilibrium between the multiple aims of design. For example, students can either reduce all redundant components in pursuit of maximizing space,

ESSAYS

or implement some kind of space articulation to achieve specific spatiality. Beginning with material and structural requisitions, the optimization process of the architectural assembly will be eventually driven by multiple factors towards the singularity of the topological space consisting of all the formal possibilities.

In the dialectic relationships between tectonics, structure and construction, construction process itself also plays important role to help students understand the materiality of the architectural assembly so as making decisions in the optimization process. Meanwhile, through the rapid construction of CNC machines, digital technologies could form a reciprocal feedback loop between virtual design and physical construction in real-time. In this way, just like how construction process shapes creativity in the traditional crafts, the construction process based on digital technology is not only for testing whether the virtual form can be materialized, but also to regain the important role of embodiment in the conception of space. Students would have embodied spatial experience on the materiality of architectural assembly and be informed back in the optimization process in virtual environment. Eventually, the integrated teaching method involving tectonics, structure and construction can correlate rule-based design technique with subjective sensibility, forming adaptability to complex design aims. In this way, the limited scale of digital fabrication tools could be transcended. Digital fabrication installations, which have emerged widely in the architecture schools around the world in past 20 years, may not only refer to a kind of demonstration for constructing complex architectural assembly, but also become a mediated way of inspiring new sensibility on architectural space and spatiality.

1. Robin Evans, *The Projective Cast: Architecture and Its Three Geometries* (Cambridge: The MIT Press, 2000), 113-21.

2. Andy Clark, *Natural-Born Cyborgs: Minds, Technologies, and the Future of Human Intelligence* (Oxford: Oxford University Press, 2003).

3. Katherine Hayles, *How We Became Posthuman: Virtual Bodies in Cybernetics Literature and Informatics* (Chicago: University of Chicago Press, 1999).

4. Mario Carpo, *The Alphabet and the Algorithm* (Cambridge: The MIT Press, 2001).

5   Martin Heidegger, *The Question Concerning Technology and Other Essays*, trans. William Lovitt (New York: Harper and Row, 1977), 3-35.

6   Antoine Picon, "From Authorship to Ownership," *Architectural Design* 5 (September/October 2016), 36-41.

7   Eduard F. Sekler, "Structure, Construction, Tectonics," in *Structure in Art and Science* (London: Studio Vista, 1964), 89-95.

PEDAGOGY

MATTER AGGREGATION

Description

Over the last 20 years, digital technology has cultivated a significant paradigm shift in architectural research and practice. New "tools" for architectural design and construction have been constantly invented and reinvented under human-machine collaborations, seeking new ways of constructing complex forms. These tools (machines), originating from the physical understanding of the material, and freeing architects from the technological limitation in the past, are now showing their great influence on the design-to-construction methodology in contemporary practice. Within the human-machine collaborations cultivated in the digital age, craft and materials are playing an increasingly important role in forming various ways of matter aggregation for architecture. By combining digital tools with craft, the dialog between emerging digital technology and material culture has brought the potential for forming unprecedented spatial affects.

Under these premises, this studio seeks new value for wood craft in contemporary architectural design. The construction techniques found in wood architecture and artifacts possess special ways of aggregating material together. The studio integrates explorations of these crafts with digital fabrication technique, establishing a digital crafting as a new field in contemporary practice. By associating digital craft with its produced spatiality, the studio will draw a series of spatial propositions for a 400 sqm museum in the Westbund art district of Shanghai.

Specifically, the studio will explore the computational mechanisms and diagrammatic grammar within these craft-based aggregation systems, paying close attention to geometrical configurations, material effects and fabrication details and will take advantage of these qualities to produce a unique spatiality. In doing so, the studio will be organized into three phases—matter iteration, matter performance and matter sensibility. The first phase is to identify and analyze aggregation systems within crafts, and to propose initial geometrical porotypes in the context of digital crafting. The second phase is to develop variations of the prototype aggregations in association with digital tools, proposing a particular spatiality in the architectural scenario. The third phase explores how aggregated tectonics can cultivate sensual interventions for both the spatial and temporal dimensions of architecture. In responding to the specific architectural context/purpose of a building, material-based crafts will be the driving factors for the generative architectural design, bringing together phenomenological experience with new tectonic culture in the digital age.

PEDAGOGY

Learning Objectives

This studio explores and experiments with materials, crafts and digital fabrication techniques to develop a design methodology of matter aggregation, in which construction research and spatial investigation inform each other for developing an architectural proposal.

- Students will develop a comprehensive understanding on wood crafts, especially their geometrical configurations in association with aggregation mechanism.

- Students will develop a productive design method that uses materials and crafts as the formal repertoire to explore spatial possibilities.

- Students will learn to integrate digital fabrication with building construction method, developing understandings on the relationships between tectonic culture and spatial experience.

Instructional Methods

This studio integrates lectures, desk critics and fabrication experiments together to explore how the digital crafts could offer new spatiality to the architecture in the contemporary age. In doing so, the studio will be organized into two parallel but mutually relevant parts. The first part consists of a series of exercises on using digital techniques to reinvent wood crafts and to produce unique architectural prototypes. The second part is a site-specific architectural project, in which the spatial prototypes developed in the first part will become the driving factor for architectural design.

Course Outline

[Topic/Goals]

PHASE 01: Matter Iteration | Endless Space

Through a series of introductory lectures, the students will be asked to identify and research on a series of crafts in the wood architecture/ artifacts around world, and use digital tools to conduct experiments on the fabrication mechanism embodied in the craft-material relationship. In this phase, the students will particularly focus on the geometrical system of matter aggregation in wood crafts—how two wood components are jointed together and how the joint can be iterated into an aggregation system. Based on the research on crafts, the students will propose, develop and test out new form system by using digital fabrication technology, to generate the initial prototypes for an endless space.

PHASE 02: Matter Performance | Scaleless Space

Through a series of exercises on digital modeling tools, the students will be asked to take spatial scale into their consideration in developing the aggregation system. The students will use digital tools to generatively transform the initial geometry into spatial prototype, forming transitions from aggregated matter to aggregated space. By introducing various performances of the aggregation geometry, the students will be asked to explore unique spatial configurations in responding to the given architectural scenario, developing the spatial proposition for their original investigation of the building site.

PHASE 03: Matter Sensibility | Formless Space

Students will focus on synthesizing the developed geometrical system with contemporary building construction technique, developing unique tectonic cultures in digital craftsmanship. By integrating the spatial explorations with real building construction scenario, the students will be asked to further articulate the spatial prototype in association with specific materials, joints and construction systems in architectural environment, speculating the sensual interventions of digital craftsmanship on both spatial and temporal dimensions of contemporary architecture.

PRECEDENTIAL
RESEARCH

01 / Research on Crafts

AXONOMETRIC DRAWING

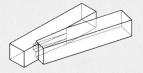

FABRICATION PROCESS

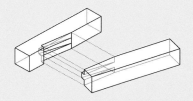

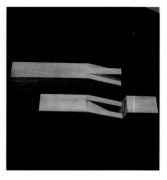

© The Art of Japanese Joinery by Kiyosi Seike

Kashigi-oire: Notched Mortise and Tenon

Nita Wareechatchai

Kashigi-orie is an angled notched mortise and tenon joint originating in Japan. This type of joint is useful for the reinforcing of eccentrically curved beams that connect to posts at sharp angles. Using this joint, carpenters may reinforce beams by adding diagonal bracing or by connecting a more horizontal beam to the curved beam.

O2 / Research on Joint Prototypes

COMPONENT TYPES

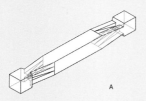

A

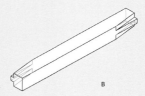

B

JOINT TYPES

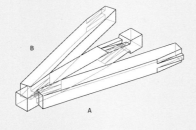

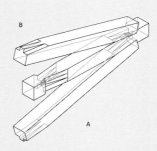

JOINT TRANSLATIONS

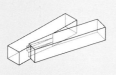

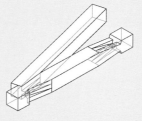

03 / Research on Aggregation System

AGGREGATION GRAMMERS

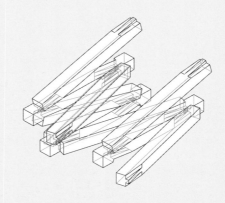

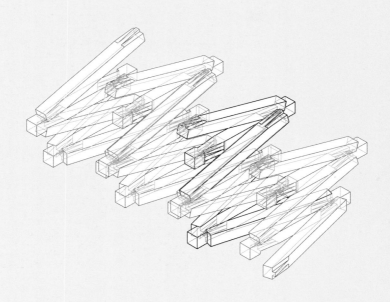

O4 / Form
Prototype

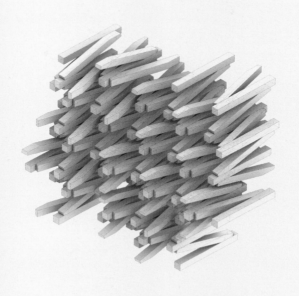

01 / Research on Crafts

AXONOMETRIC DRAWING

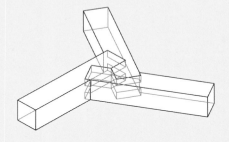

FABRICATION PROCESS

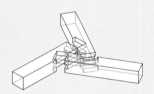 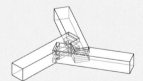 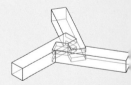

© Lee Sinclair Design Co.

Three-Way Bridle Joinery

Nita Wareechatchai

The bridle joint is a type of mortise and tenon joint whose length of tenon is the equivalent to its depth of mortise. This creates a strong joint and exposes the end grain of the wood members. The bridle joint has more adjoining surface area between members which allows for a strong joint when glued together. The specific three-way joint studied here originates from an Australian furniture company that uses the joint in the base of one of their side table designs.

O2 / **Research on Joint Prototypes**

COMPONENT TYPES

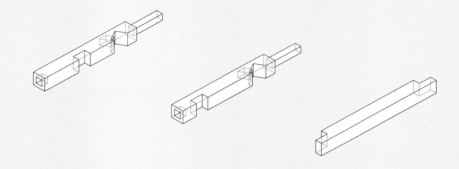

JOINT TYPES

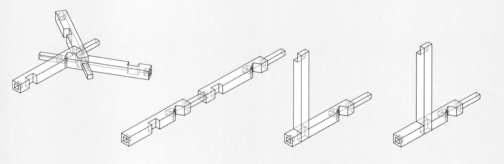

JOINT TRANSLATIONS

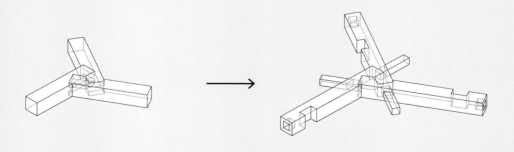

O3 / Research on Aggregation System

AGGREGATION GRAMMERS

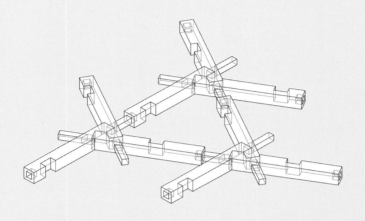

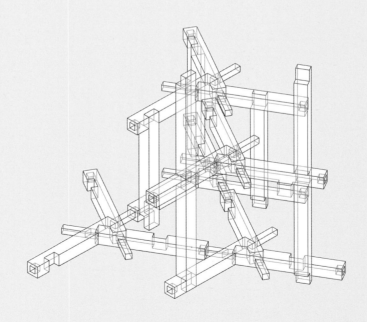

04 / Form
Prototype

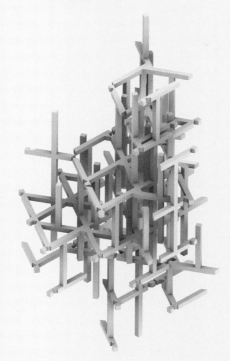

MATTER AGGREGATION

O1 / **Research on Crafts**

AXONOMETRIC DRAWING

FABRICATION PROCESS

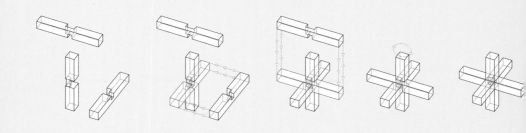

Burr Puzzle

Nita Wareechatchai

The burr puzzle is a mechanical puzzle made of notched sticks that interlock to form a three-dimensional unit. The historical origins of these types of joints are obscure, but some believe they may have originated in China due to the style of these joints.

52

O2 / **Research on Joint Prototypes**

COMPONENT TYPES

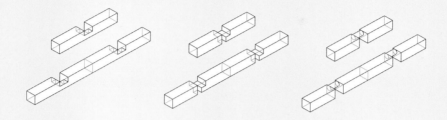

JOINT TYPES

JOINT TRANSLATIONS

03 / Research on Aggregation System

AGGREGATION GRAMMERS

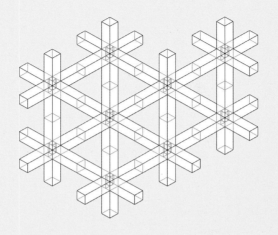

O4 / **Form
Prototype**

O1 / Research on Crafts

AXONOMETRIC DRAWING

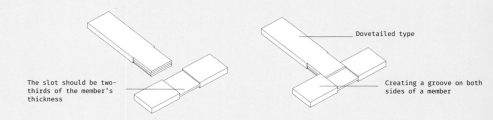

The slot should be two-thirds of the member's thickness

Dovetailed type

Creating a groove on both sides of a member

FABRICATION PROCESS

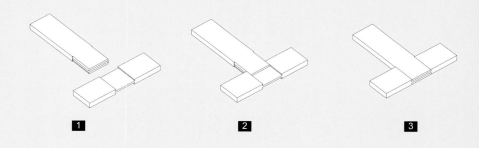

1

2

3

Source: https://www.
popularwoodworking.com/
woodworking-blogs/t-bridle-joint/

T-Bridle Joint

Xuting Jin

T-bridle joint is one subtype of the bridle joint, which is similar to a group of a mortise and tenon, connecting the end of one part to the middle of another part. But the difference is that "T-bridle joint is formed by creating a groove on both sides of a member and inserting it into the slotted end of an open-ended slip joint". It is commonly applied into traditional timber framing because of its great performance in "load-carrying capacity".

02 / **Research on Joint Prototypes**

COMPONENT TYPES

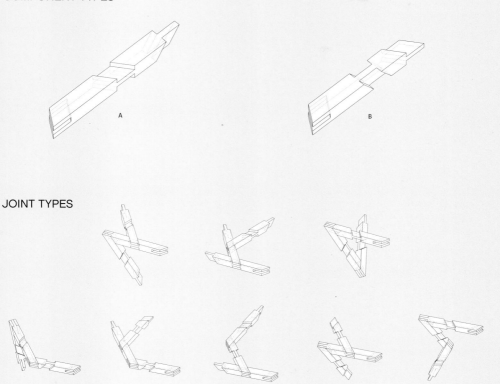

JOINT TYPES

JOINT TRANSLATIONS

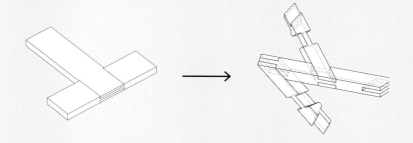

03 / Research on Aggregation System

AGGREGATION GRAMMERS

A+A

Part A can be connected at the middle or end with itself.

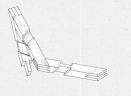

The connection types in different members are almost the same.

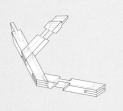

Creating rules within Part A or between Part A and B can get two types of group on the right.

O4 / **Form**
Prototype

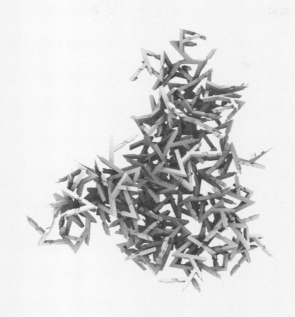

01 / Research on Crafts

AXONOMETRIC DRAWING

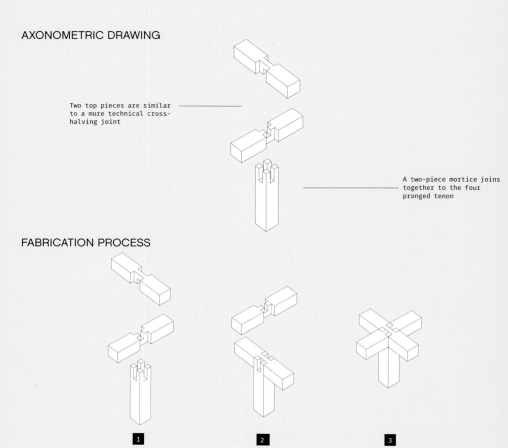

Two top pieces are similar to a more technical cross-halving joint

A two-piece mortice joins together to the four pronged tenon

FABRICATION PROCESS

1

2

3

Interlocking-Tenon Joint

Xuting Jin

This type of joint is always applied in chair and staircase construction, which can connect two or more pieces together. It includes three members coming together in three dimension. "The two top pieces are similar to a more technical cross-halving joint, which is actually a two-piece mortice that then joins together to the four pronged tenons. This joint requires fine skill and an extensive range of tools and time to create it perfectly. "

O2 / Research on Joint Prototypes

COMPONENT TYPES

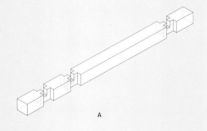

A

B

JOINT TYPES

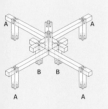

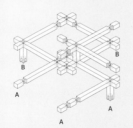

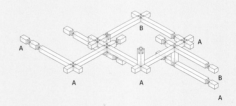

JOINT TRANSLATIONS

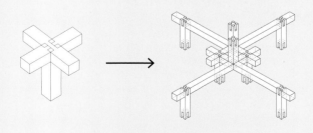

03 / Research on Aggregation System

AGGREGATION GRAMMERS

A+B

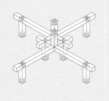
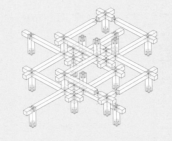

Part A is connected with itself, which constitutes a group supported by Part B.

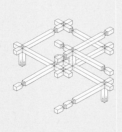
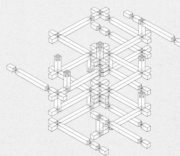

Part A is connected with itself, which constitutes a group supported by Part B.

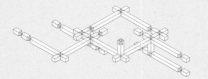

Each connection with Part A itself is supported by Part B, which is also a connection piece for another group of Part A.

04 / Form
Prototype

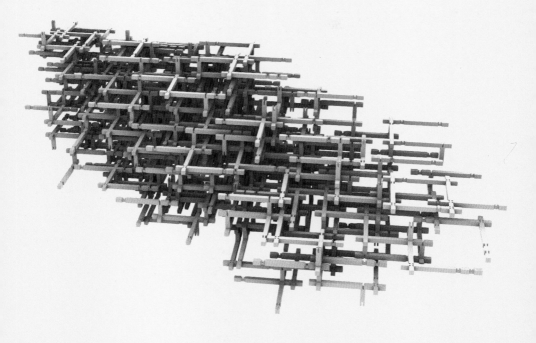

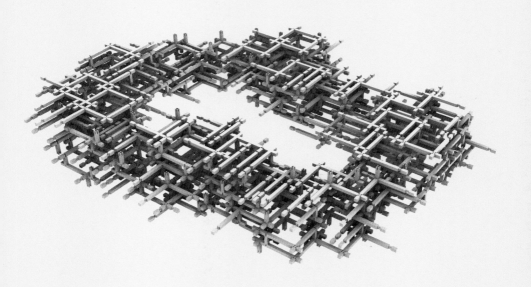

MATTER AGGREGATION

O1 / **Research on Crafts**

AXONOMETRIC DRAWING

A series of 'pins' cut to extend from the end of one board interlock with a series of 'tails' cut into the end of another board.

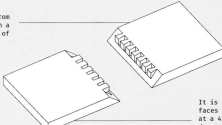

It is totally hidden from both outside faces by forming the outer edge to meet at a 45-degree angle while hiding the dovetails internally within the joint.

FABRICATION PROCESS

1

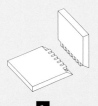
2

3

Full Blind Dovetail Joint

Xuting Jin

The type of dovetail joint is a common joinery technique in carpentry, such as furniture and cabinets, especially connecting pieces of a drawer at the side. "A series of 'pins' cut to extend from the end of one board interlock with a series of 'tails' cut into the end of another board."

The full-blind dovetail can also be called as the secret miter dovetail, which is always used in the highest class of furniture. "It offers the strength found in the dovetail joint but is totally hidden from both outside faces by forming the outer edge to meet at a 45-degree angle while hiding the dovetails internally within the joint."

64

O2 / **Research on Joint Prototypes**

COMPONENT TYPES

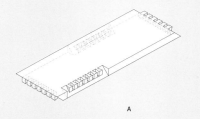

A

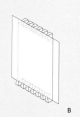

B

JOINT TYPES

JOINT TRANSLATIONS

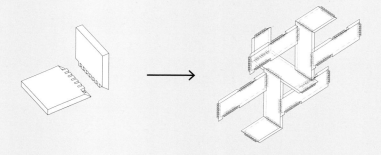

03 / Research on Aggregation System

AGGREGATION GRAMMERS

A+B

Each side of part A has one joint. Two of them are connected with itself, and the left are connected with part B.

Each side of part A has one joint. Three of them are connected with part B, and the left one is connected with itself.

Part A has four connection divided on each side, which allows to develop the aggregation on four direction. Part B becomes a connection member for each group.

O4 / **Form Prototype**

MATTER AGGREGATION

01 / Research on Crafts

AXONOMETRIC DRAWING

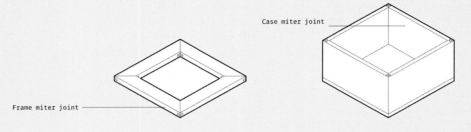

Case miter joint

Frame miter joint

FABRICATION PROCESS

1   2   1   2

Splined Miter Joint

Linxi Lu

The splined miter joint provides reinforcement to mitered corners in frames, small boxes, and large cases.

Source:
https://www.woodworkersjournal.com/
making-spline-miter-box-joints/

O2 / Research on Joint Prototypes

COMPONENT TYPES

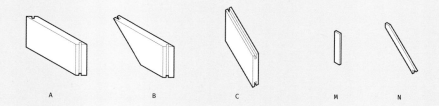

A   B   C   M   N

JOINT TYPES

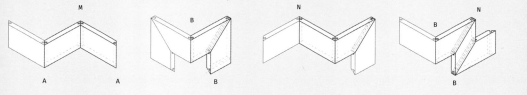

JOINT TRANSLATIONS

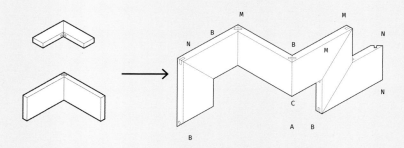

69

03 / Research on Aggregation System

AGGREGATION GRAMMERS

A+B+M

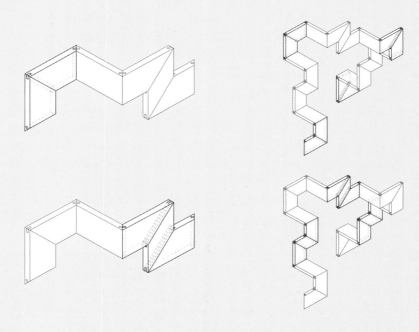

B+C+N

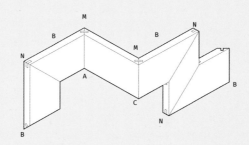

04 / Form
Prototype

MATTER AGGREGATION

01 / Research on Crafts

AXONOMETRIC DRAWING

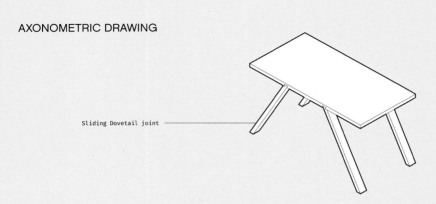

Sliding Dovetail joint

FABRICATION PROCESS

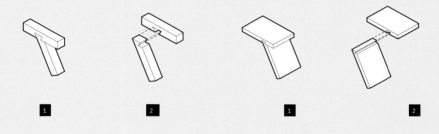

1   2   1   2

Sliding Dovetail Joint

Linxi Lu

The sliding dovetail is a method of joining two boards at right angles, where the intersection occurs within the field of one of the boards, that is not at the end. This joint provides the interlocking strength of a dovetail. Sliding dovetails are assembled by sliding the tail into the socket.

Source:
https://interiorsnow.wordpress.com/
2013/11/05/details-10-timber-fixings/

O2 / **Research on Joint Prototypes**

COMPONENT TYPES

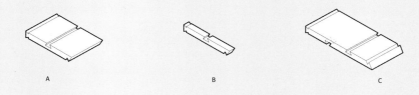

A

B

C

JOINT TYPES

A

B

C

JOINT TRANSLATIONS

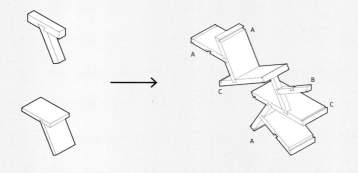

03 / **Research on Aggregation System**

AGGREGATION GRAMMERS

A+C

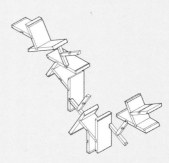

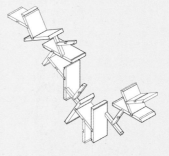

B+C

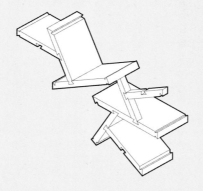

O4 / **Form**
Prototype

O1 / Research on Crafts

AXONOMETRIC DRAWING

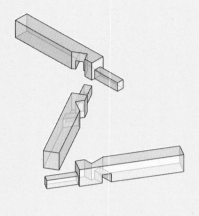

1

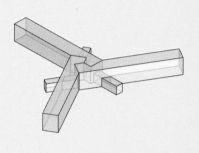

2

Three-way Doweled Splice

Andrew Spears

This joint is one of my own adaptation, though it draws upon instances such as those to the left. The inspiration is to be able to securely join three timbers at their ends, though this joint design in particular features a rotated end, so that multiple turns can be made in an overall geometry.

O2 / **Research on Joint Prototypes**

COMPONENT TYPES

JOINT TYPES

1

2

3

JOINT TRANSLATIONS

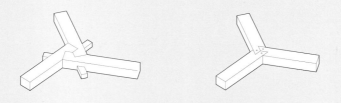

03 / Research on Aggregation System

AGGREGATION GRAMMERS

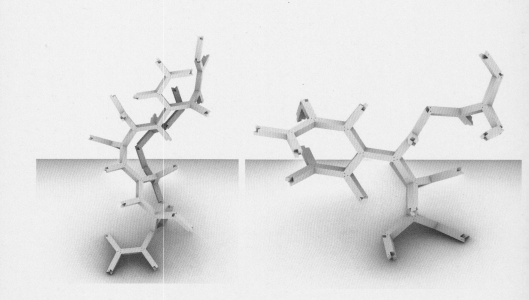

O4 / Form
Prototype

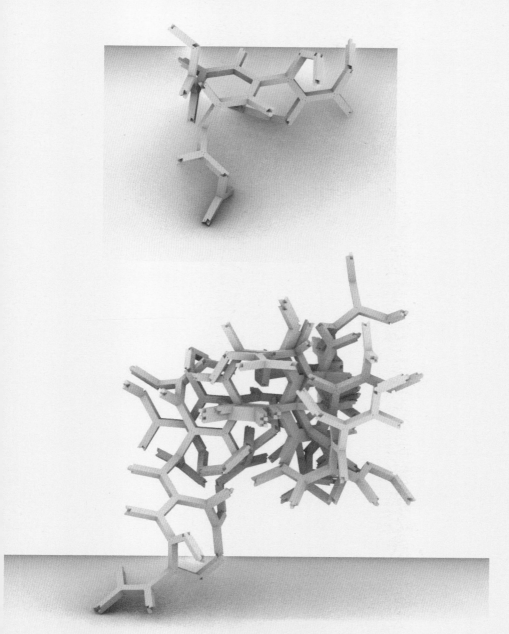

01 / Research on Crafts

AXONOMETRIC DRAWING

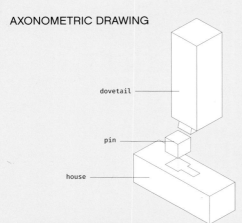

dovetail

pin

house

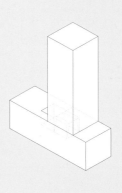

FABRICATION PROCESS

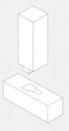

Housed Dovetail

Ryan Shih

The joint focuses on a dovetail that slides into its respective counterpart, which is then locked into place with an additional block. The block is typically fabricated so that it's permanent once placed within the joint. In essence, it's an altered tenon and mortise joint that utilises a locking and pin mechanism to hold the joint in place.

Wood Joints in Classical Japanese
Architecture
Sumiyoshi + Matsui

O2 / Research on Joint Prototypes

COMPONENT TYPES

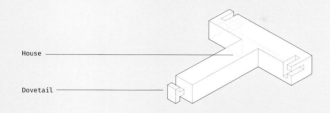

House

Dovetail

JOINT TYPES

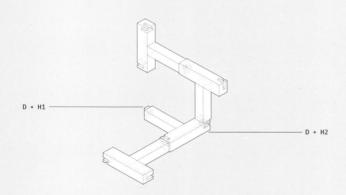

D + H1

D + H2

JOINT TRANSLATIONS

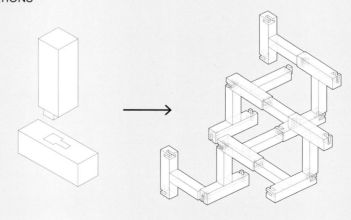

O3 / **Research on Aggregation System**

AGGREGATION GRAMMERS

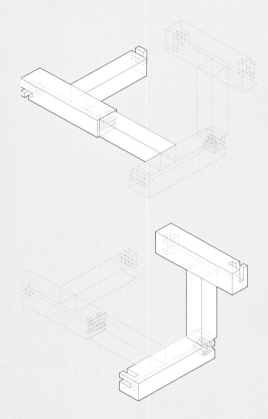

The orthagonal nature of the joint allows for the house to be placed anywhere on a 3 dimensional axis, placed a the end of a piece.

The sliding mechanism of the dovetail, while not locked in this aggregation, can be further edited to push into the material.

The directionality of the dovetail determines a particularly specific function in which the joint effectively aggregates. This results in a uniform total aggregation, with only one or to variant components.

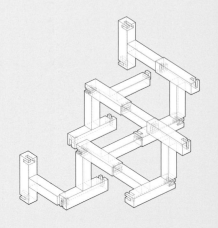

O4 / Form Prototype

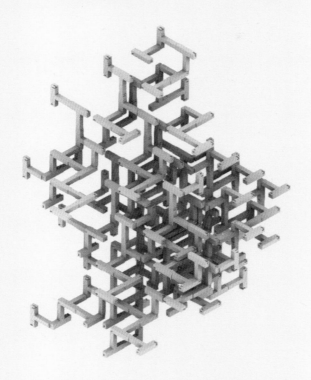

O1 / **Research on Crafts**

AXONOMETRIC DRAWING

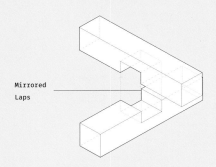

Mirrored
Laps

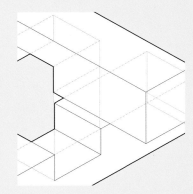

FABRICATION PROCESS

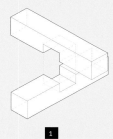

1

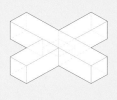

2

Lap Joint

Ryan Shih

The lap joint is perhaps the most basic, yet most universal and versatile joint of them all. It simply consists of two negatives that nest within each other, and are typically orthogonal negatives that mirror each other.

O2 / Research on Joint Prototypes

COMPONENT TYPES

Lap Part A

Lap Part B

JOINT TYPES

A2+ B1

A4+ B2

A1+ B2

JOINT TRANSLATIONS

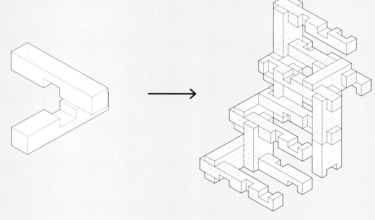

03 / **Research on Aggregation System**

AGGREGATION GRAMMERS

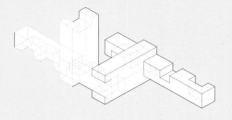

The orthagonal nature of the joint allows for the house to be placed anywhere on a 3 dimensional axis, placed a the end of a piece.

The lap joint comfortably sits spaced apart, translating a consistent gap between the joint.

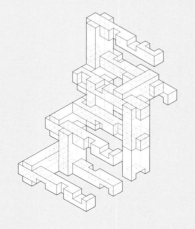

The density of the joints and proximity of the laps create a dynamic, yet densly aggregated cluster, with clear hierarchy.

O4 / **Form Prototype**

01 / Research on Crafts

AXONOMETRIC DRAWING

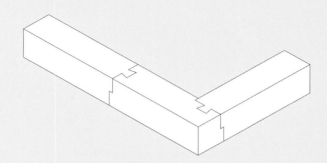

FABRICATION PROCESS

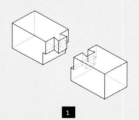

1

2

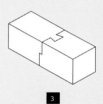

3

Stepped Dovetail

Sarah Miller

This joint is primarily used to join groundsills. The traditional dovetail is only carved into the joint at half depth and flares out at the end to serve as a locking mechanism. The other half of the joint is a flat and fits into the corresponding ledge. The joint fits together with no twisting or pins placed through. The primary use of this joint is to hold in tension as there are no pins holding the two pieces snuggly together.

credits info: Sumiyoshi, Torashichi, and Gengo Matsui. Wood Joints in Classical Japanese Architecture. S.l.: J. Nagy, 1991.

O2 / **Research on Joint Prototypes**

COMPONENT TYPES

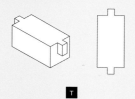

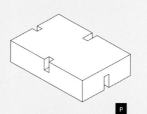

JOINT TYPES

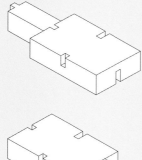

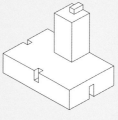

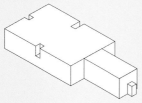

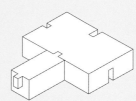

JOINT TRANSLATIONS

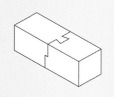

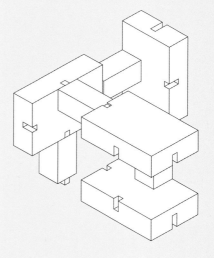

89

03 / Research on Aggregation System

AGGREGATION GRAMMERS

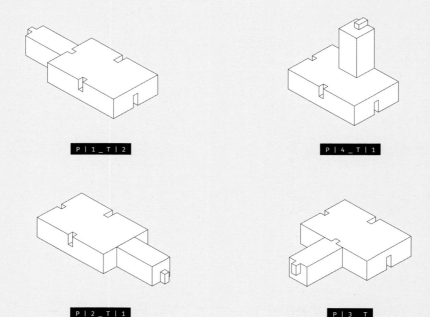

P | 1 _ T | 2

P | 4 _ T | 1

P | 2 _ T | 1

P | 3 _ T

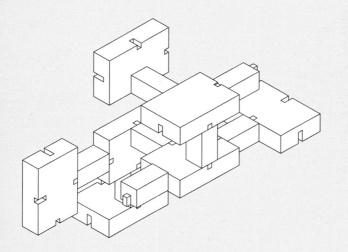

This aggregation focuses on utilizing different connection points within the context of the traditional dovetail joint. By employing different orientations and directions for connection, it allows for an increasingly dynamic modular structure. The components can be altered to bring about new types of aggregations though the current study focuses on a large, shelf-like component.

04 / Form
Prototype Render

O5 / Form
Prototype

O5 / Form
Prototype

05 / Form
Prototype

O5 / **Form Prototype**

01 / **Research on Crafts**

AXONOMETRIC DRAWING

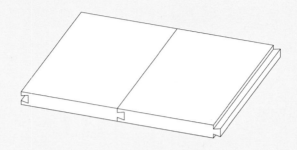

FABRICATION PROCESS

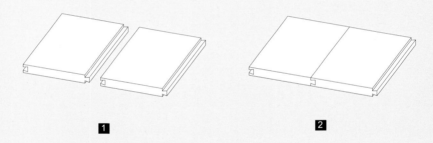

Sliding Dovetail Variation

Sihan Lai

Positive end and negative side of the part allows rotaiton and variation.

O2 / Research on Joint Prototypes

COMPONENT TYPES

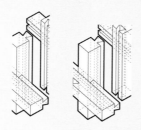

JOINT TYPES

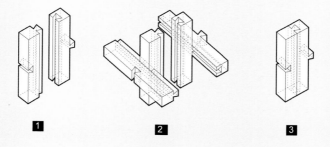

JOINT TRANSLATIONS

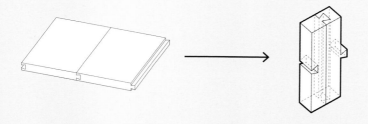

03 / Research on Aggregation System

AGGREGATION GRAMMERS

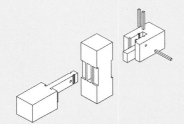

This connecting joint is used to join two beams on opposing sides of a column. The beams slide through the column and interlock. The beam with the longer tenon portion is inserted first with the second following until both tenon pieces fit in the assembly snugly. Though it is a tight connection joint, two keys and a draw pin are driven into the assembly to further strengthen it against tensile failure. The keys and pin are dependent upon one another and require the assembly to be fully tightened prior to insertion.

04 / Form
Prototype

01 / Research on Crafts

AXONOMETRIC DRAWING

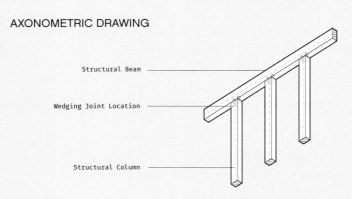

Structural Beam

Wedging Joint Location

Structural Column

FABRICATION PROCESS

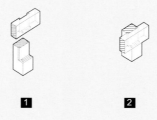

1 **2**

Source: Dorian Bracht, "Joint Venture"
Episode 42

Mortise + Tenon + Dovetail

Jake Gianni

This joint combination, like the one before, is designed to handle the transfer bewteen beams and columns.Unlike the previous joint however, the sliding dovetail allows for more stablilization against torsional forces within the structure.The Mortise + Tenon+ Dovetail combination, at least in the images I've seen, implies that the column will be wider than the beam it is engaging with, which is not the case with the blind wedging joint.

02 / Research on Joint Prototypes

COMPONENT TYPES

JOINT TYPES

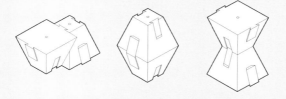

JOINT TRANSLATIONS

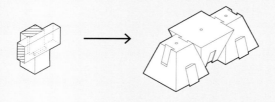

03 / Research on Aggregation System

AGGREGATION GRAMMERS

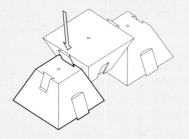

The predominant connection for this joint is made by sliding one piece into the side of another. Because of the dovetail, two pieces at a time must be slid into place.

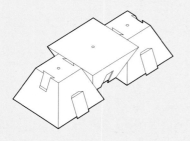

This group of three becomes the common "unit" of the aggregation. From here, it can be stacked.

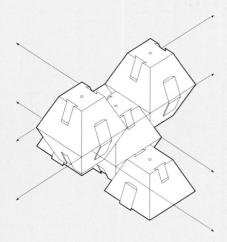

Because of the mirrored/truncated nature of the units, this aggregation cannot move in the X and Y directions on the same plane. Therefore, the layout to the right is the primary means of expanding the aggregation in different directions. This in turn indicates that the units will have to be able to act as cantilevers at some points within the aggregation.

O4 / **Form Prototype**

01 / Research on Crafts

AXONOMETRIC DRAWING

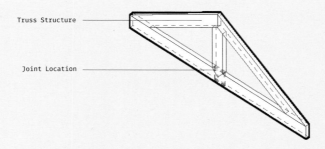

Truss Structure ────

Joint Location ────

FABRICATION PROCESS

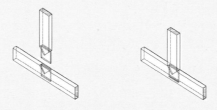

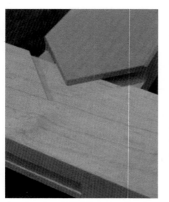

Through Tenon + Miter

Jake Gianni

Though there wasn't much online in the way of this joint's historical use, it's not much of a stretch to imagine that this could be uesd within a truss system. Because the angle can vary to about 45 degrees in either direction, the joint could definitely help define the lateral bracing within a structure. Due to the lack of a dovetail or other geometry to hold the thorugh tenon in place (other than maybe wedges), it likely would need some aid to be utilized effectively in tension.

Source: Dorian Bracht, "Joint Venture"
Episode 6

O2 / Research on Joint Prototypes

COMPONENT TYPES

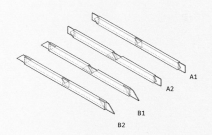

A1
A2
B1
B2

JOINT TYPES

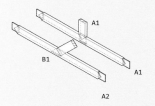

A1
B1
A1
A2

JOINT TRANSLATIONS

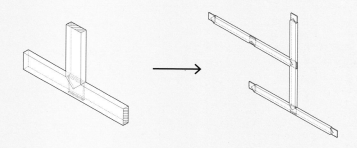

03 / Research on Aggregation System

AGGREGATION GRAMMERS

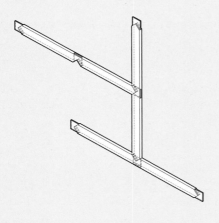

The predominant connection for this joint is made by inserting the tenon through a receiving void in the center of each unit.

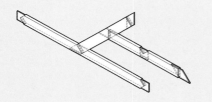

The 45 degree angle through tenon allows for a break in the otherwise rectalinair nature of the aggregation.

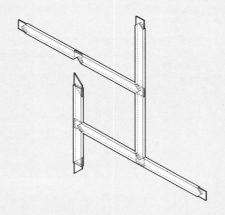

To ensure full connections are possible, the lengths of each piece will need to be defined so that a 45, 45, 90 triangle is attainable. While planar in form, aggregations of this joint are capable of taking.

04 / **Form**
Prototype

MATTER AGGREGATION

01 / Research on Crafts

AXONOMETRIC DRAWING

Beam Element

Truss Element

Joint Connection

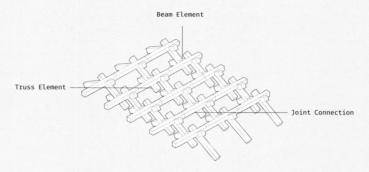

FABRICATION PROCESS

1

2

3

Source: The joint Book

Hip Rafter Joint

Zhenkang Zhai

This kind of joint composed with there pieces with different directions. It just like two pieces of truss and support elements to support the beam element. The most interesting part of this joint is that, it has three directions, xyz, so with this joint, it can create any shape what you like. Besides, the weakness of this joint is very stable to support the force and it can transfer the forces in the diagonal direction. But if it overturn the piece in the middle will easily break. Also if the holes for this two pieces is big and connection will easily break. Also the force can transfer from X-direction to Y-direction and can support the force from the Z-direction.

O2 / **Research on Joint Prototypes**

COMPONENT TYPES

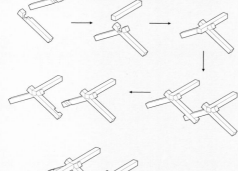

JOINT TYPES

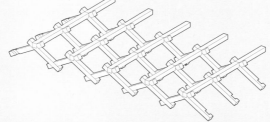

JOINT TRANSLATIONS

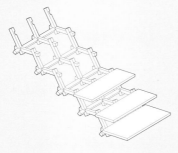

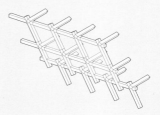

03 / Research on Aggregation System

AGGREGATION GRAMMERS

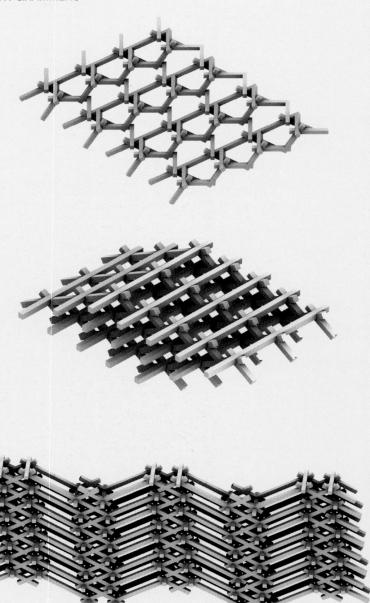

O4 / Form
Prototype

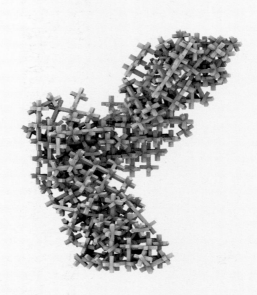

MATTER AGGREGATION

01 / Research on Crafts

AXONOMETRIC DRAWING

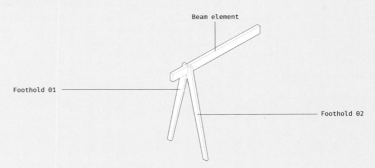

Beam element

Foothold 01

Foothold 02

FABRICATION PROCESS

1

2

3

Credits info: The joint Book

The Tongue-and-Groove

Zhenkang Zhai

Have you worked with wainscoting, interlocking siding, or laminate floors before? Then you've probably seen a tongue-and-groove wood joint. This tends to be a wood joint used to hold two boards together on their edges, rather than along the ends. One end is curved so that it has a protruding piece (the tongue), and the matched piece is carved with a recession (the groove). They should interlock and fit snugly together.

Sometimes the tongue and groove are cut at a slight angle so that the boards must be attached at an angle and then pushed down to "lock" in place-mainly laminate floors these days.

02 / **Research on Joint Prototypes**

COMPONENT TYPES

JOINT TYPES

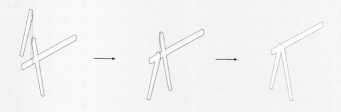

JOINT TRANSLATIONS

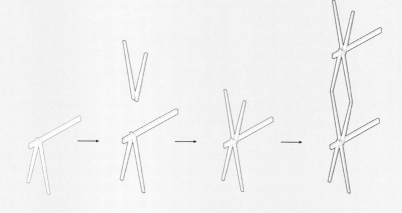

03 / **Research on Aggregation System**

AGGREGATION GRAMMERS

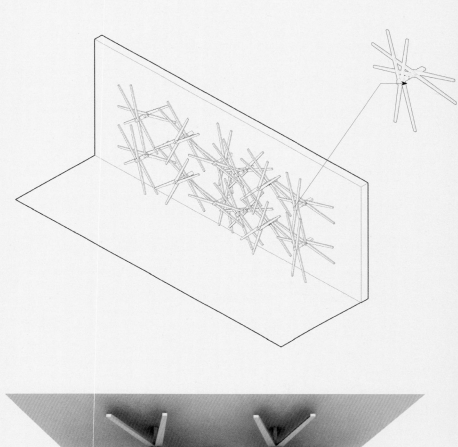

O4 / Form
Prototype

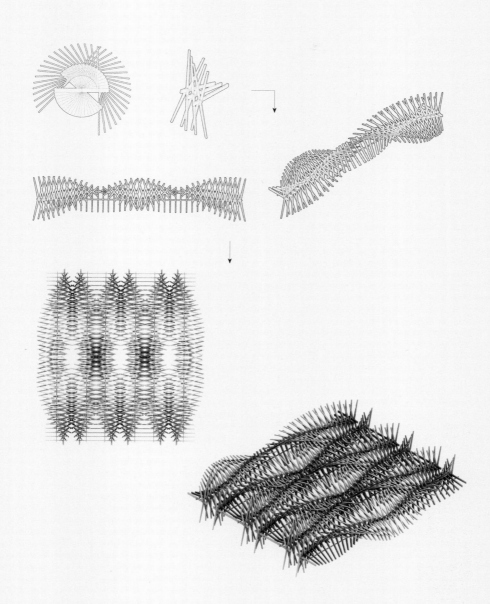

01 / **Research on Crafts**

AXONOMETRIC DRAWING

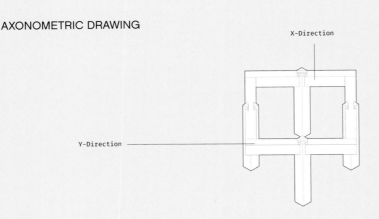

X-Direction

Y-Direction

FABRICATION PROCESS

1　　　**2**

The Dado Wood

Zhenkang Zhai

Using a dado is a very functional and strong method for connecting two pieces of stock. Once you learn how to cut a dado, you'll find these woodworking joints especially useful when building cabinets or bookshelves.

A dado is a groove cut into one piece of wood into which another piece of wood ill fit snugly. For instance, when building a bookshelf using ¾ "thick stock, one would cut a ¾" wide groove into the shelf standard and then glue the shelf into the groove.

Credits info: The joint Book

116

O2 / **Research on Joint Prototypes**

COMPONENT TYPES

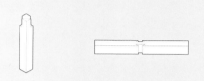

JOINT TYPES

JOINT TRANSLATIONS

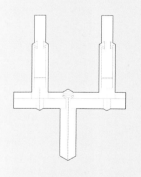

03 / Research on Aggregation System

AGGREGATION GRAMMERS

04 / Form Prototype

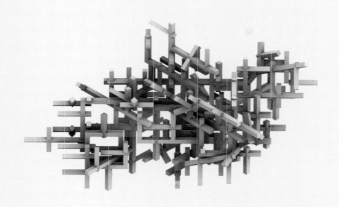

MATTER AGGREGATION

01 / Research on Crafts

AXONOMETRIC DRAWING

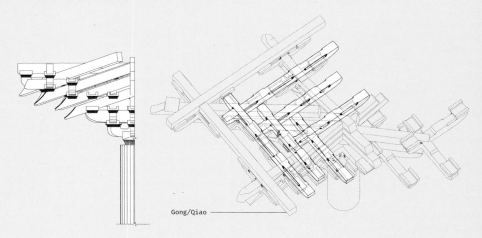

Gong/Qiao

FABRICATION PROCESS

 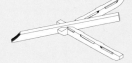 

Source: Klaus Zwerger. Wood and Wood Joints: Building Traditions of Europe, Japan and China

Foguang si Dongda dian—Dougong

Jiawei Luo

Craft has been serving as a structural system in traditional eastern asian arthitecture in China, Korea, Japan. It is a vertical load-resistant system that well-used in wooden building. After development of thousands years, it also became a decoration part of building in the area. it is the most famous and most important part of the ancient Chinese architecture.

O2 / Research on Joint Prototypes

COMPONENT TYPES

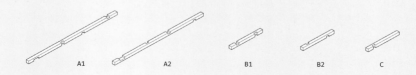

A1   A2   B1   B2   C

JOINT TYPES

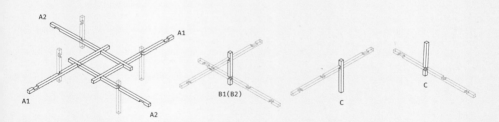

A2   A1   B1(B2)   C   C
A1   A2

JOINT TRANSLATIONS

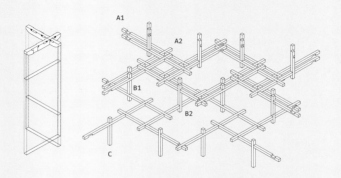

A1   A2   B1   B2   C

O3 / Research on Aggregation System

AGGREGATION GRAMMERS

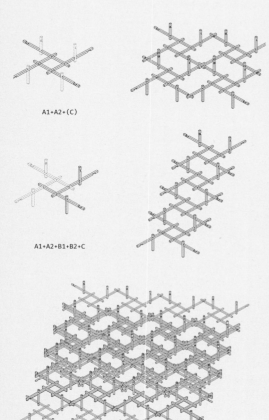

A1+A2+(C)

A1 + A2 + (C)

This redesigned joint is a kind of circulation in 2D scale that may served and facade or horizontal element of structural and architectural idea. It also can be bended in different curve rate to suit for various facades.

A1+A2+B1+B2+C

A1 + A2 + B1 + B2 + C

This redesigned joint enables the fabricated system to grow up in 3D scale and meanwhile it may keep the posibility of expanding in the 2D surface.

A1+A2+B1+B2+C

This system is formed by all the 5 pieces. the 5 pieces could be served as a single unit to initiate the design and it share the common structural sytem. Because of the joint location demension differences the system is not totally vertical, instead, it breaks the traditional trend of the joints and creates a new graceful perspective of joints system.

122

04 / **Form Prototype**

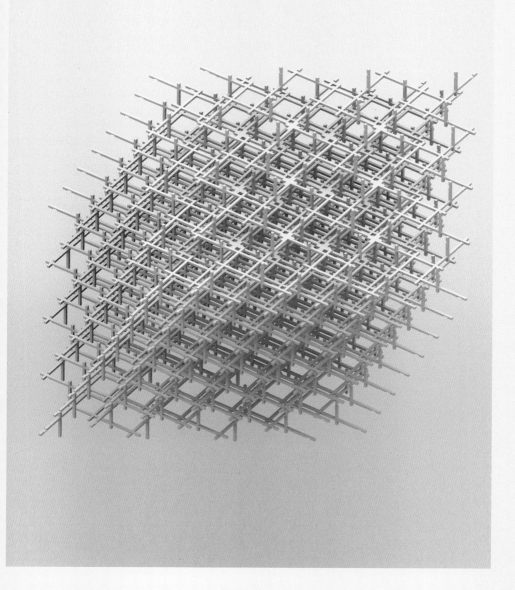

O1 / **Research on Crafts**

AXONOMETRIC DRAWING

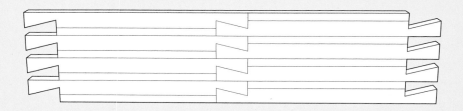

FABRICATION PROCESS

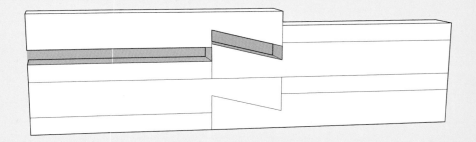

credits info: *The Language of Wood:*
Wood in Finnish Sculpture, Design, and
Architecture

Horizontal Log Dovetail Joint

Kelsea Champ

This traditional Finnish building technique is composed of dovetail joints at the neck of a log that connect the end of a log to the beginning of another. By shaping the neck of the log, there is an improvement in gripping that allows for a layering of materials. This horizontal log technique came from the same jointing principles that can be used at various scales.

O2 / Research on Joint Prototypes

COMPONENT TYPES

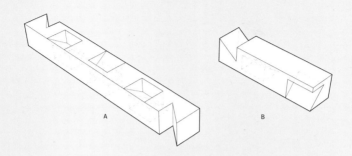

JOINT TYPES

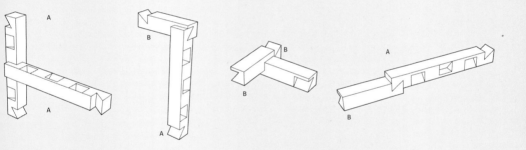

JOINT TRANSLATIONS

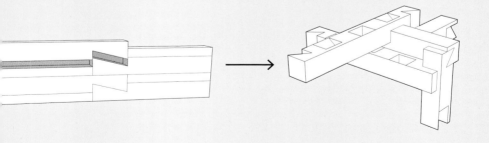

O3 / **Form
Prototype**

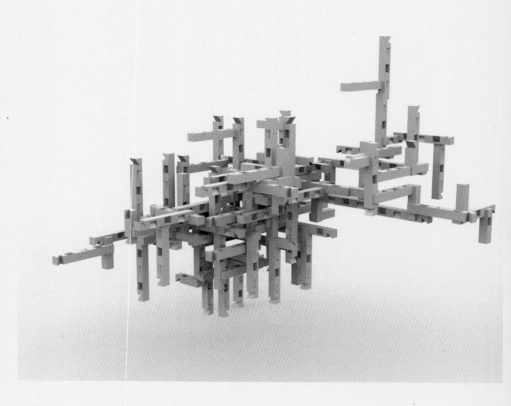

O4 / Form
Prototype

MATTER AGGREGATION

01 / Research on Crafts

AXONOMETRIC DRAWING

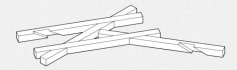

FABRICATION PROCESS

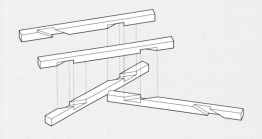

Halved Joint

Diyu Zheng

The corner of the bell-tower in Malé Ozorovce, Slovakia. The inclined columns with halved joints are assembled togethe in certain degree.

O2 / **Research on Joint Prototypes**

COMPONENT TYPES

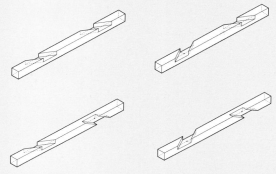

JOINT TYPES

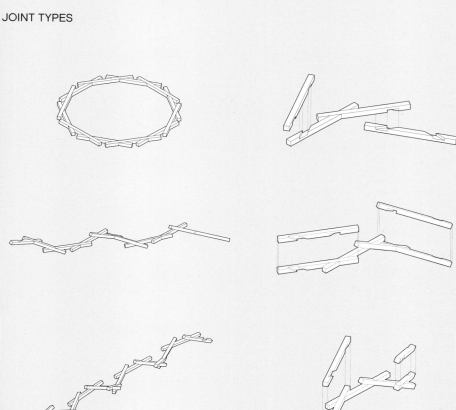

03 / Research on Aggregation System

AGGREGATION GRAMMERS

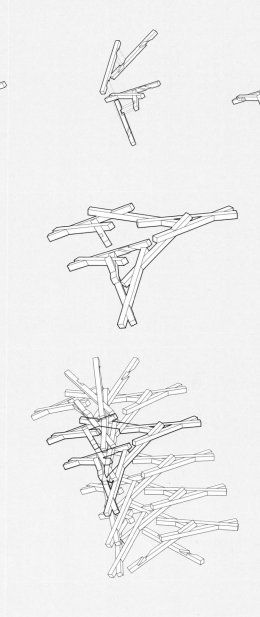

O4 / Form
Prototype

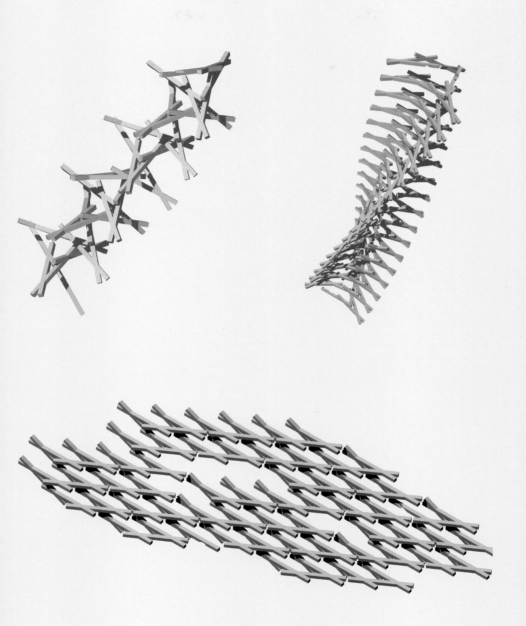

SELECTED BUILDING PROJECTS

SELECTED BUILDING PROJECTS

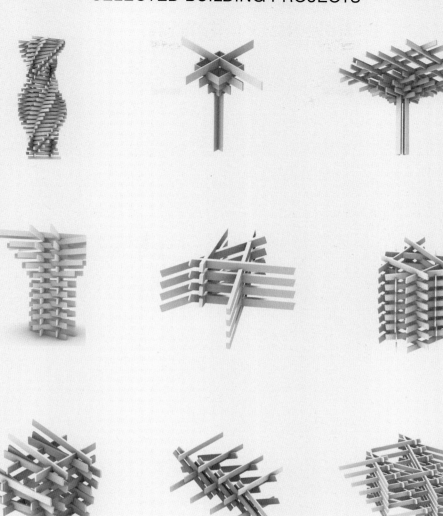

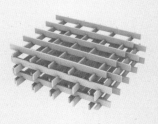

Jake Gianni, Qiuheng Xu, Zhenkang Zhai

PROJECT 01

Jake Gianni
Qiuheng Xu
Zhenkang Zhai

SELECTED BUILDING PROJECTS

Matter Iteration / **PROTOTYPE STUDY**

JOINT SECTION

JOINT DETAIL

AGREGATION FORM EXPLORATION-SIZE

AGREGATION FORM EXPLORATION-PLAN

AGREGATION FORM EXPLORATION-SECTION

AGREGATION FORM EXPLORATION-SPACE

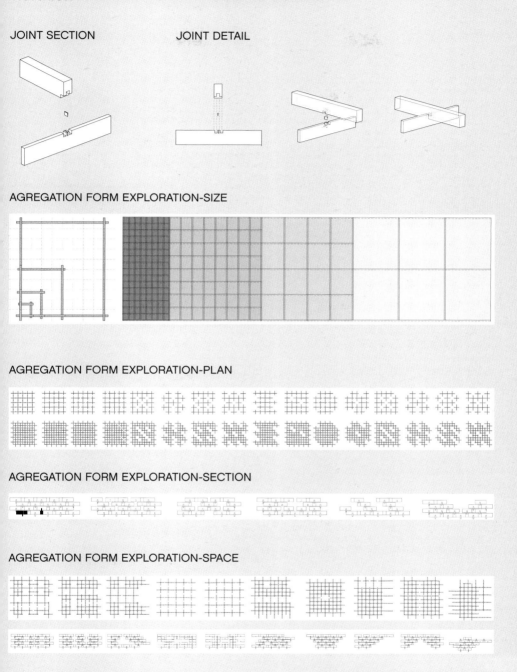

MATTER AGGREGATION

Matter Performance / **STRUCTURAL OPTIMIZATION**

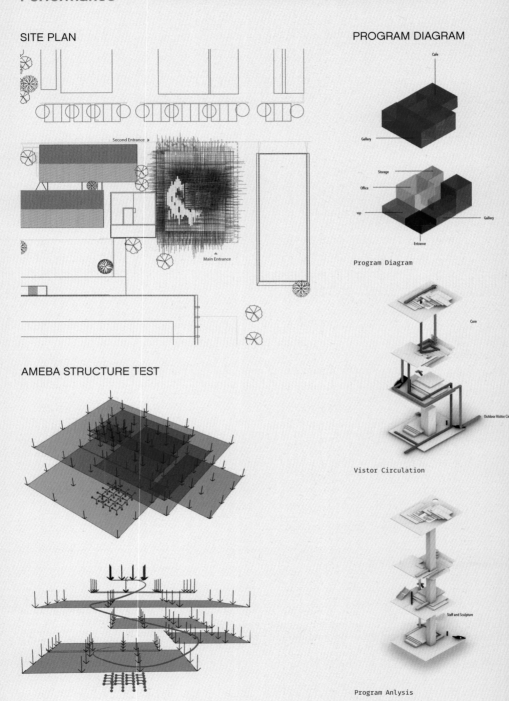

SITE PLAN

Second Entrance ▶

Main Entrance

AMEBA STRUCTURE TEST

PROGRAM DIAGRAM

Cafe

Gallery

Storage

Office

hop

Gallery

Entrance

Program Diagram

Core

Outdoor Visitor Cir

Vistor Circulation

Staff and Sculpture

Program Anlysis

SELECTED BUILDING PROJECTS

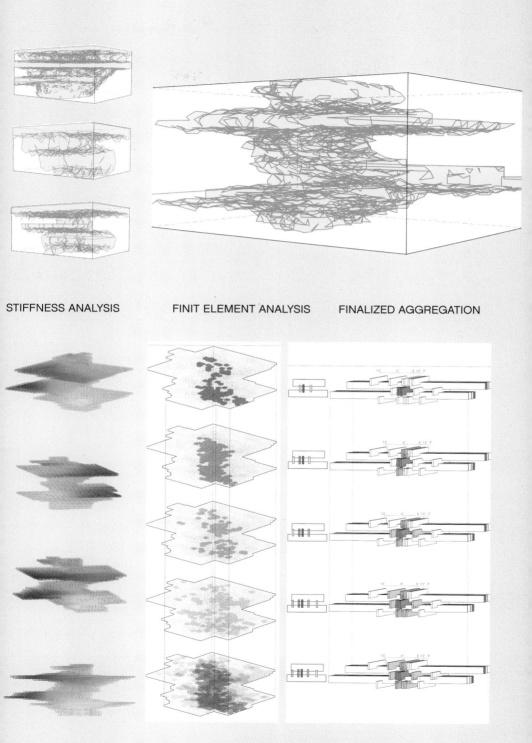

STIFFNESS ANALYSIS   FINIT ELEMENT ANALYSIS   FINALIZED AGGREGATION

EXPLODED AGGREGATION

EXPLODED AXONMATRIC

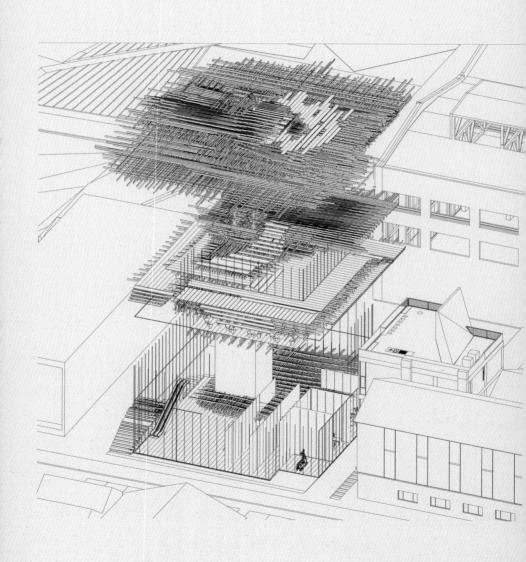

SELECTED BUILDING PROJECTS

NORTH-EAST SECTION

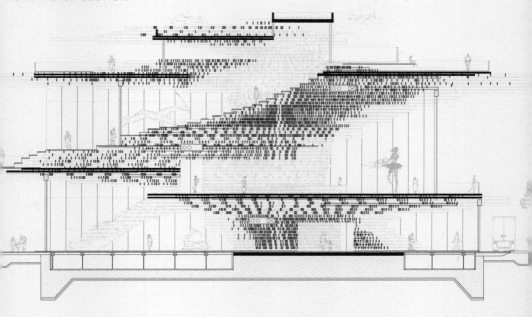

PERSPECTIVE FACADE

MATTER AGGREGATION

DETAIL RENDERING ROOD

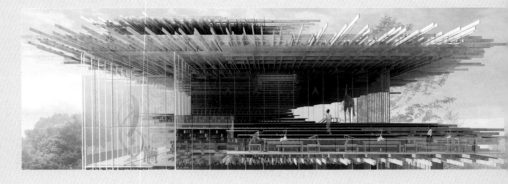

GROUND PLAN

SECOND PLAN

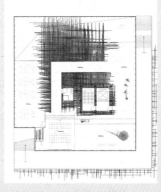

THIRD PLAN

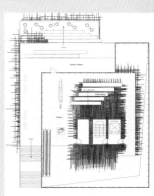

CONSTRUCTION PHASE

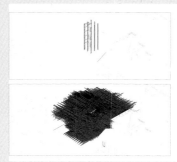

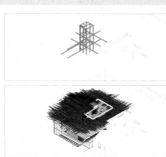

SELECTED BUILDING PROJECTS

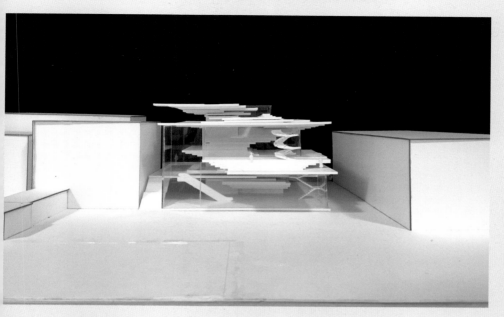

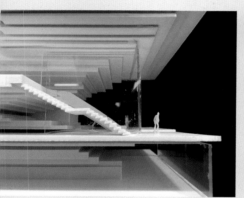

ENTERANCE-SECTION PERSPECTIVE

Main Entrance

Shanghai Dream Center

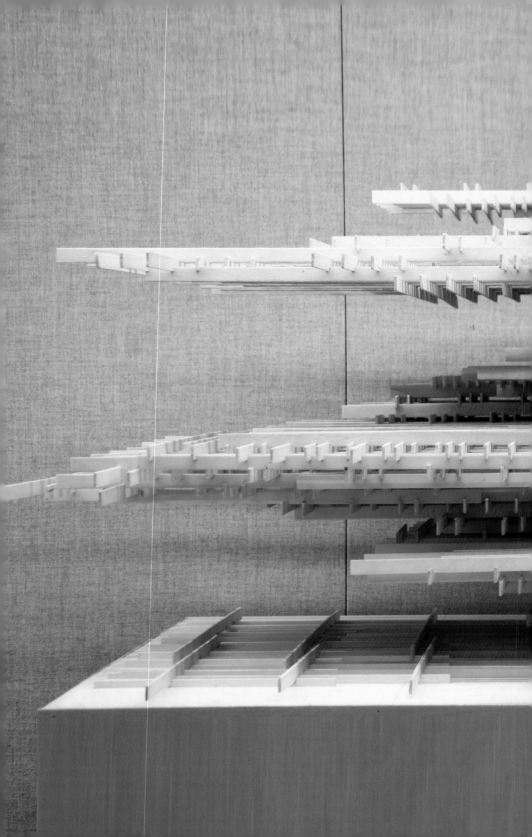

PROJECT 02

Gene Jones
Sihan Lai
Paige Simmons

SELECTED BUILDING PROJECTS

Matter Iteration / **PROTOTYPE STUDY**

JOINT DIMENSIONS

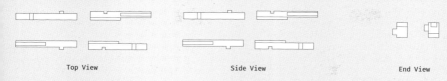

Top View   Side View   End View

PRECEDENT STUDIES: THE SLIDING HALF DOVETAILED JOINT

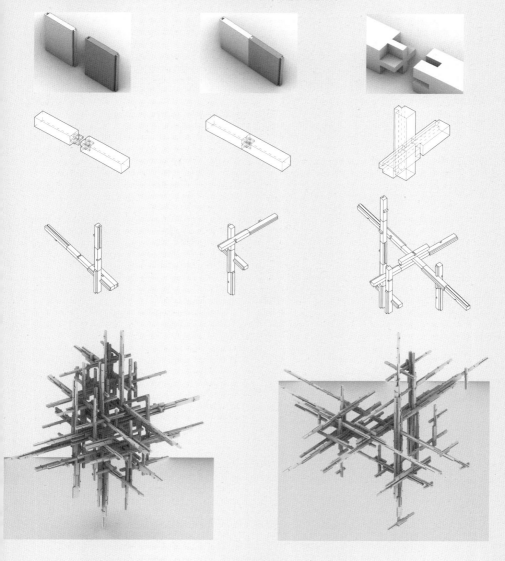

MATTER AGGREGATION

JOINT CONNECTIONS

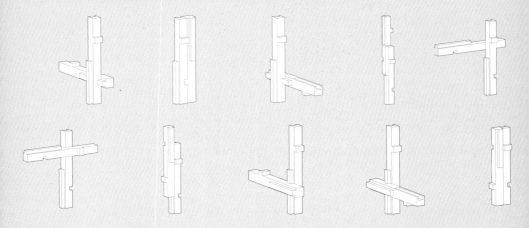

SAMPLE AGGREGATIONS

5 Parts Aggregation

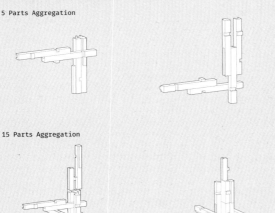

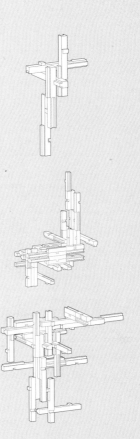

15 Parts Aggregation

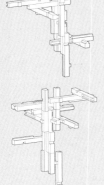

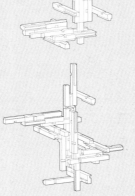

SELECTED BUILDING PROJECTS

Matter
Performance / **STRUCTURAL OPTIMIZATION**

JOINT TO AGGREGATION

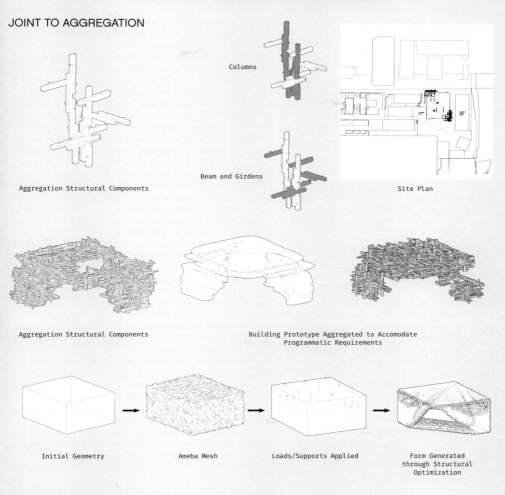

Columns

Aggregation Structural Components

Beam and Girdens

Site Plan

Aggregation Structural Components

Building Prototype Aggregated to Accomodate Programmatic Requirements

Initial Geometry

Ameba Mesh

Loads/Supports Applied

Form Generated through Structural Optimization

PREVIOUS AMEBA FORM-FINDING EXPLORATIONS

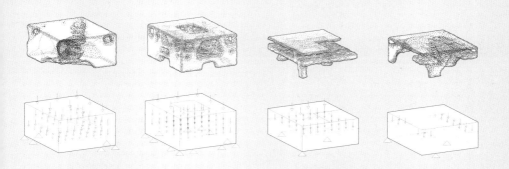

**Matter
Sensibility** / **FULL-SCALE FABRICATION**

Aggregation
Prototype Column

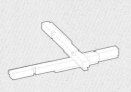

Aggregation Prototype
Beam Girder Connection

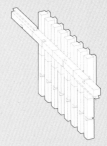

Aggregation
Prototype Wall

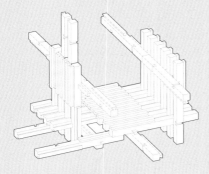

Aggregation Prototype
Corridor

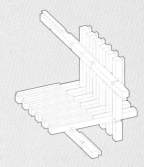

Aggregation Prototype
Wall—Floor Connection

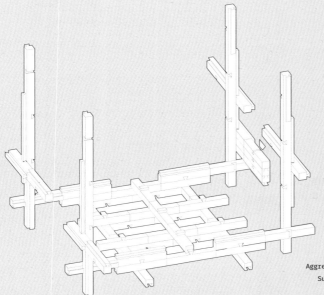

Aggregation Prototype
Suspended Floor

SELECTED BUILDING PROJECTS

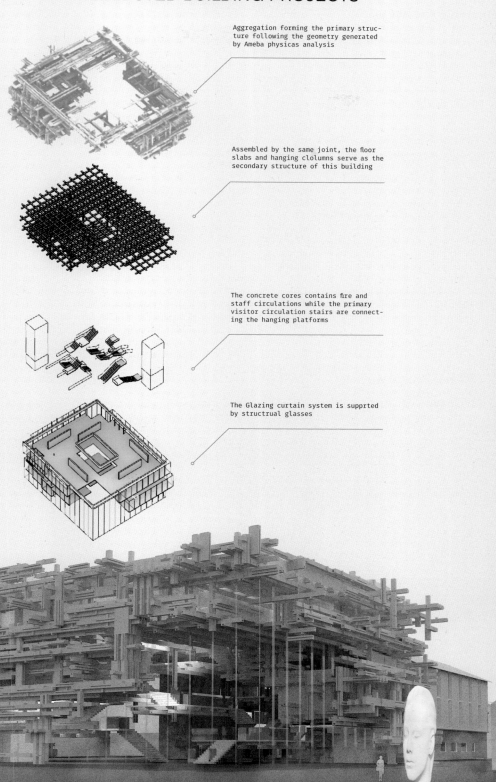

Aggregation forming the primary structure following the geometry generated by Ameba physicas analysis

Assembled by the same joint, the floor slabs and hanging clolumns serve as the secondary structure of this building

The concrete cores contains fire and staff circulations while the primary visitor circulation stairs are connecting the hanging platforms

The Glazing curtain system is supprted by structrual glasses

MATTER AGGREGATION

SECTION

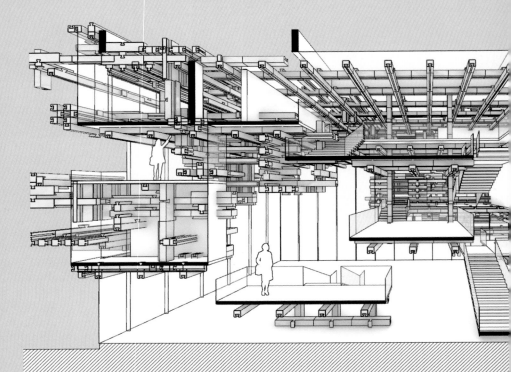

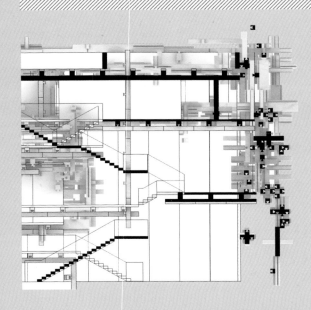

DETAILED SECTION

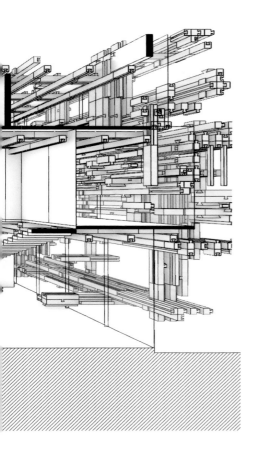

GROUND LEVEL

MID LEVEL

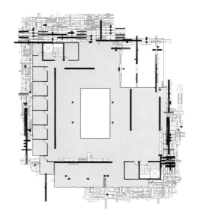

UPPER LEVEL

MATTER AGGREGATION

SEQUENTIAL SECTIONS

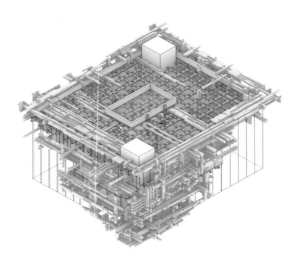

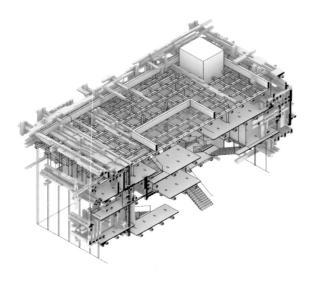

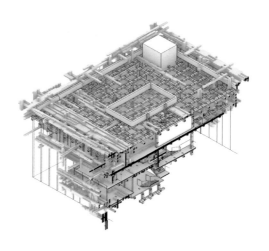

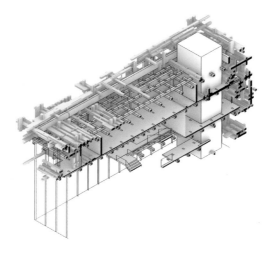

PROJECT 03

Xuting Jin
Linxi Lu
Nita Wareechatchai

**Matter
Iteration** / **PROTOTYPE STUDY**

CRAFTS TO JOINTS

Components

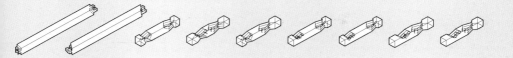

Joints

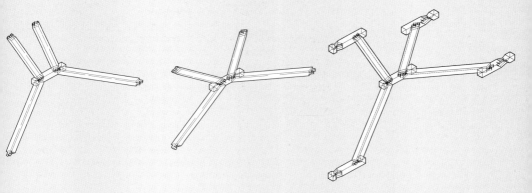

AGGREGATION DIAGRAMS

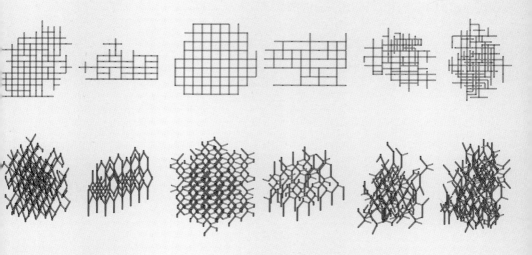

MATTER AGGREGATION

Matter Performance / **STRUCTURAL OPTIMIZATION**

JOINTS TO AGGREGATION

Site Plan

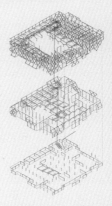

Visitor Circulation Diagram

Staff Circulation Diagram

STRUCTURAL FORM-FINDING PROCESS

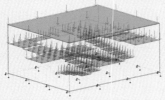

Support and load set

BOUNDARY SET ITERATIONS

Leave entry and the whole courtyard unoccupiable

Leave entry and part of courtyard with larger height unoccupiable

AMEBA STRUCTURE FORM

Final ameba form

Ameba Form Iterations

STRUCTURAL WALL SYSTEM

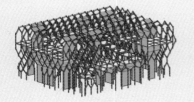

Based on ameba form

ROOF SYSTEM

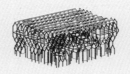

Roof frame and the relationship with structural walls

CLT boards as main roof structure

SELECTED BUILDING PROJECTS

Matter
Sensibility / **FULL-SCALE FABRICATION**

PROGRAM DIAGRAM

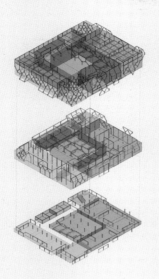

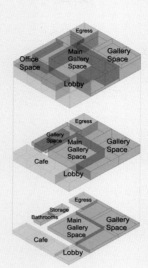

AGGREGATION STRUCTURAL SYSTEM

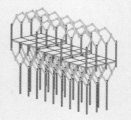

Wall System

Ceiling System

Ceiling System

MATTER AGGREGATION

AGGREGATION TO STRUCTURE SYSTEM

SELECTED BUILDING PROJECTS

SUPPORT AND LOAD SET

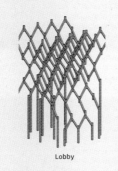

Lobby

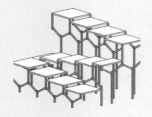

Platform of Small Size

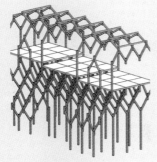

Platform of Large Size

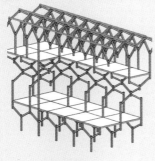

Corridor

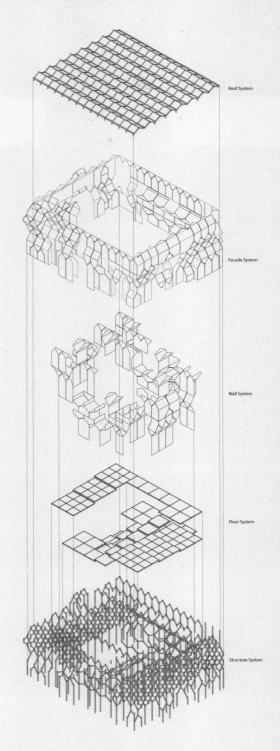

Roof System

Facade System

Wall System

Floor System

Structure System

MATTER AGGREGATION

STRUCTURE SYSTEM TO ARCHITECTURE

Ground Floor Plan 1:100

2nd Floor Plan 1:100

3rd Floor Plan 1:100

SECTION

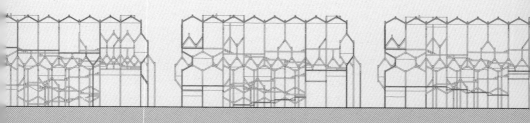

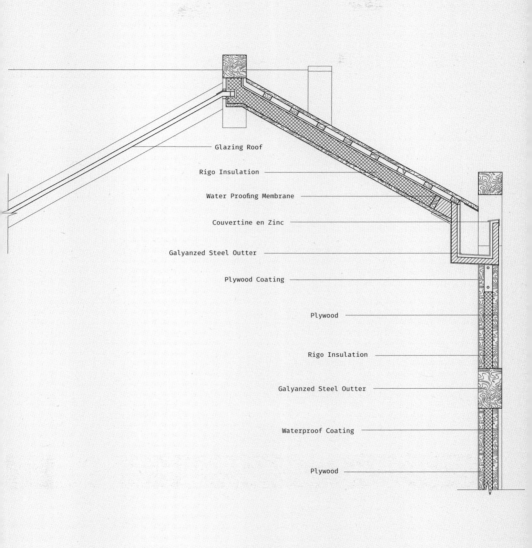

Glazing Roof

Rigo Insulation

Water Proofing Membrane

Couvertine en Zinc

Galyanzed Steel Outter

Plywood Coating

Plywood

Rigo Insulation

Galyanzed Steel Outter

Waterproof Coating

Plywood

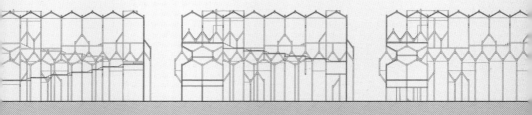

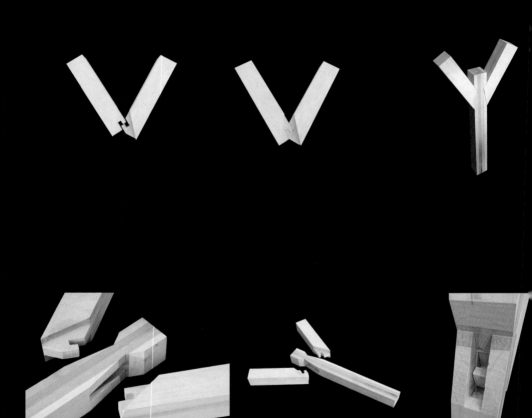

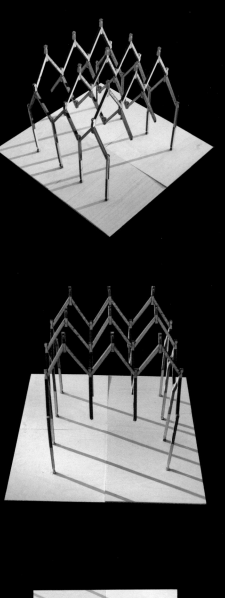

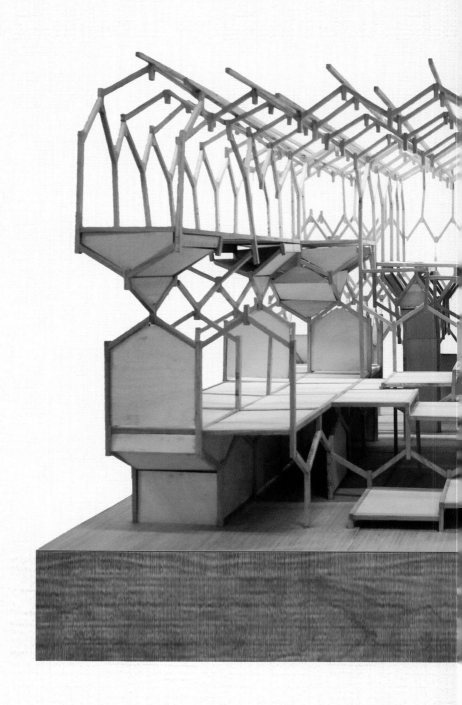

WORKING
PROCESS AND FINAL
REVIEW

Jake Gianni, Qiuheng Xu, Zhenkang Zhai

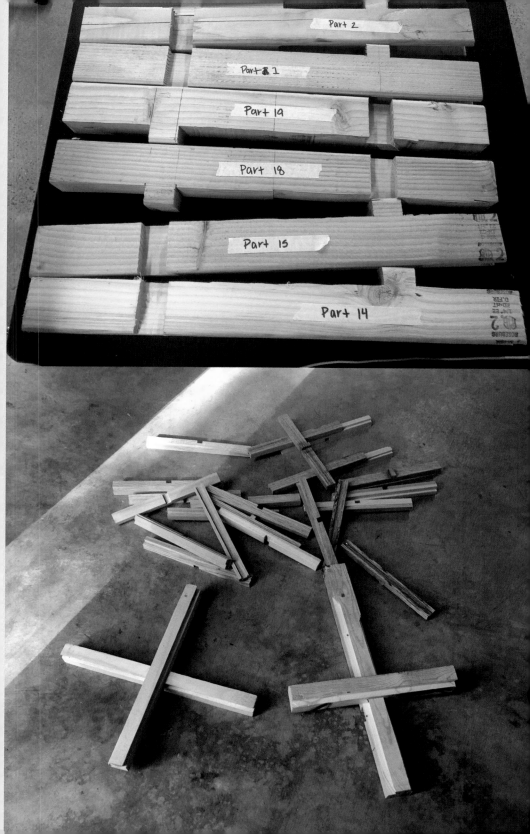

Gene Jones, Sihan Lao, Paige Simmons

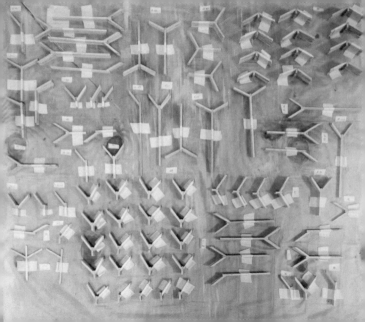

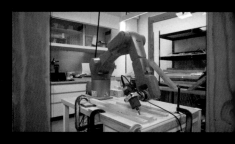

Xuting Jin, Linxi Lu, Nita Wareechatchai

Kelsea Champ, Jiawei Luo, Diyu Zheng

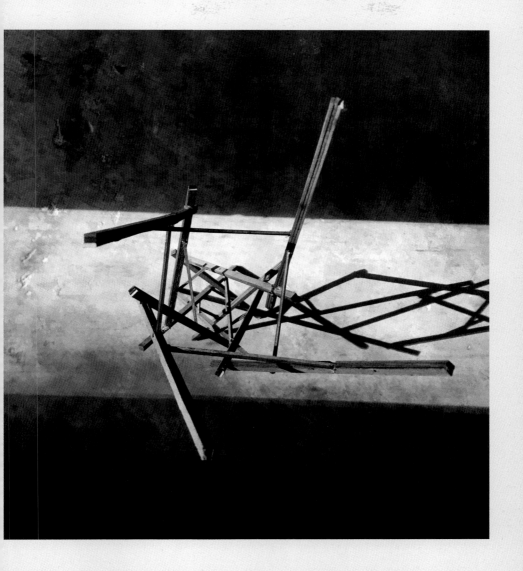

Sarah Miller, Ryan Shih, Andrew Spears

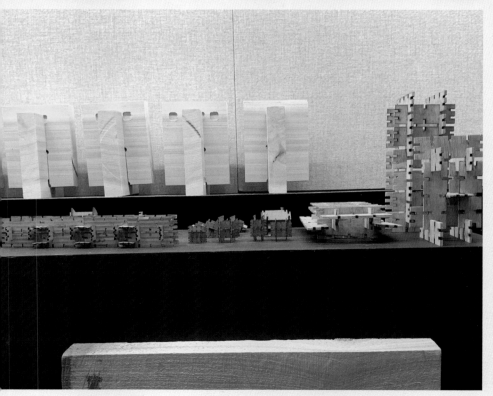

MATTER AGGREGATION
@ UABB 2019

NOMADIC WOOD (right image)
By Philip F. Yuan

DESIGN TEAM:
Hua Chai
Junbang Su
Yujun Mao
Chao Yan

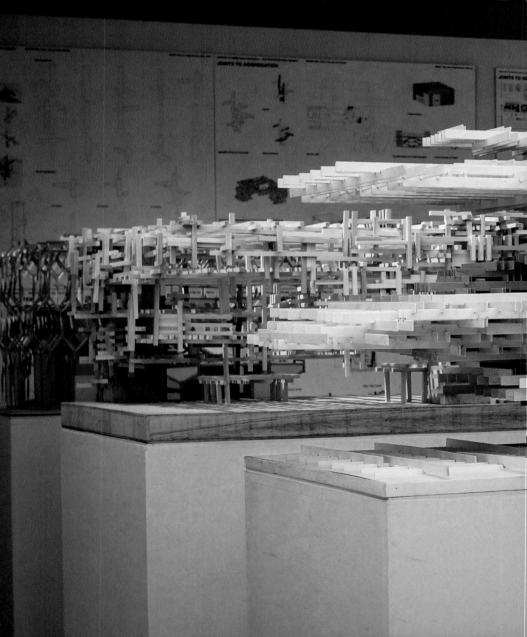

设计智能 DESIGN

MATTER AGGREGATION
University of Virginia
School of Architecture
ARCH 4010/ALAR 8010 Design/Research Studio

INSTRUCTORS
Philip F. Yuan
Lucia Phinney

TEACHING ASSISTANT
Chao Yan

STUDENTS
Kelsea Champ
Jake Gianni
Xuting Jin
Gene Jones
Sihan Lai
Linxi Lu
Jiawei Luo
Sarah Miller
Ryan Shih
Paige Simmons
Andrew Spears
Nita Wareechatchai
Qiuheng Xu
Zhenkang Zhai
Diyu Zheng

ACKNOWLEDGEMENTS
Thanks to Dean Ila Berman, Chair Felipe Correa, professor Shiqiao Li, Esther
Lorenz, Melissa Goldman and Trevor Kemp for their generous supports on this
studio. We also want to thank Robin Dripps, Meejin Yoon, Matias del Campo,
Kirk Martini, Ehsan Baharlou and all the other reviewers for their generous
comments and suggestions to the students' work.

ORO Editions
Publishers of Architecture, Art, and Design
Gordon Goff: Publisher

www.oroeditions.com
info@oroeditions.com

Published by ORO Editions

Authors: Philip F. Yuan, Lucia Phinney and Chao Yan
Preface: Ila Berman
Book Design: Jiayin Hu
Managing Editor: Jake Anderson
Executive Editor: Jialin(Crisie) Yuan

10 9 8 7 6 5 4 3 2 1 First Edition

ISBN: 978-1-951541-75-0

Color Separations and Printing: ORO Group Ltd.
Printed in China.

ORO Editions makes a continuous effort to minimize the overall carbon footprint
of its publications. As part of this goal, ORO Editions, in association with Global
ReLeaf, arranges to plant trees to replace those used in the manufacturing of
the paper produced for its books. Global ReLeaf is an international campaign
run by American Forests, one of the world's oldest nonprofit conservation
organizations. Global ReLeaf is American Forests' education and action program
that helps individuals, organizations, agencies, and corporations improve the
local and global environment by planting and caring for trees.